45337

✓ FIS

D0349231

TWO'S COMPANY

Joyce Stranger

TWO'S COMPANY

LONDON
MICHAEL JOSEPH

First published in Great Britain by
Michael Joseph Ltd
52 Bedford Square
London WC1B 3EF
1977

ISBN 0 7181 1610 0

Photoset in Baskerville eleven on twelve point
by Saildean Limited
Printed in Great Britain
by Hollen Street Press Limited, Slough

Dedicated to my mother's sisters,
Gladys and Margery, who have
me to stay every year, complete
with two dogs, which is most
noble of them.
With all my love.

Foreword

This book is about my two dogs. Those who cannot bear to read an animal story because they know it is about an animal now dead need have no fears as mine are still alive and with me.

I wrote about them because both have had problems which have, mostly, been overcome, and my experiences may help others; they may also help others not to make some of the mistakes I have made with my pair.

Janus is a Golden Retriever; he has a major fault that is inherited, but don't think that I am 'getting at' retriever breeders, as I am not. It is a breed I love and when Janus goes, I plan to buy a little bitch, but with much more knowledge than I had when I bought him.

For all that, though he is far from physically perfect, I have learned a great deal through him that I would not have learned with a very easy dog, and it is only fair to say before you begin to read, that he is not at all typical of his breed; the reasons will appear as you read.

Puma is a German Shepherd, which is the correct name for the Alsatian. She had problems too, of a different kind, as she is a very good specimen of her breed physically; her problems came through a piece of sheer bad luck when she was a pup.

The early years were far from easy, but now both dogs

7

are no longer problem dogs in the normal ways of living. Our new problems are unreal as they stem from my enjoyment of competition Obedience, and this means training dogs to a degree far above that required for a normal pet; and far below that required for a working dog like a Guide dog or a Police dog, so that sometimes when I talk of problems, I don't mean what you mean, unless you too have been bitten by the desire to gain a little of the pleasure that comes when man and animal form a working team, understanding one another, working together and achieving together, both of them using their brains in a way that is not possible in the day-to-day scramble for a living.

Breeders need not condemn me nor fear I am trying to say that the pedigree dog is unsound; I know mine is not typical, though there are others like him. But perhaps if you breed you will see from reading this that pet owners are not all sentimental fools spoiling their dogs; they ask of a dog that he should be fit to walk with them and work with them, and not a constant worry, always at the vet.

Those of us who have dogs have them for a variety of reasons; mine are companions and guards when I am alone; they protect my car when we travel; they come for long walks, and give me exercise; they distract me, so that in watching them live their lives, I forget some of the irritations of human existence, as they race across the dunes, or Janus joyously tries to carry a stick that is far too long for him, while Puma chases imaginary rabbits, and digs up invisible objects out of the sand, or just leans into the wind, and races, greyhound fast, after the shadows of speeding clouds.

A dog's life, in the best circumstances, is a very good life.

Sadly, it is a short life, but there is always the next dog to learn from, as for me, each animal is a benefit, lent briefly, from which I derive great pleasure and I could no more be without one when the present one goes, than I can cut myself off from friends because I am saddened when my friends die, leaving me a little more lonely, until one day someone else comes along, and the gap is healed.

My dogs are fun. Though in the early days I doubted that this would ever happen, as it seemed unlikely that either would survive to adulthood.

I might have given up several times, but I went on, and now, looking back, I realise how much I would have missed by despairing.

My dogs are unique; nothing like yours, and your next one will be unique too as though all dogs are dog, just as all humans are human, no two are ever alike. All the same there may be clues in these pages that will explain your dog to you, but what works for mine may never work for yours; what works for Janus doesn't work for Puma and would never have worked with my fantastic old dog, Turk. And that's what's so fascinating about dogs.

Chapter 1

My teachers at school laughed at me, because, when asked what I wanted to do when I grew up, I always gave the same answer. My friends might choose to be nurses, teachers, mothers, or secretaries, but I was going to write, and I was going to breed dogs.

Neither met with approval. Writing was a very precarious way of earning a living and breeding dogs was just plain silly. My statements were greeted with tolerant smiles and those infuriating glances that adults exchange when a child says something they think rather absurd.

I doubt if any of them realised that I wasn't *going* to write; I *was* writing. I spent most of my waking hours improving on the books I read; I spent some extremely tedious maths and geography lessons working my way in imagination up impassable mountains or over appalling terrain, always accompanied by my dog.

My childhood life was enlivened by dogs; some of them memorable; others not. Paddy, the only long-legged Sealyham in the world, disgraced herself by biting my aunt, who picked up her newborn pups. Paddy vanished, along with the pups as my father wouldn't tolerate a dog that bit; we didn't speak to him for a month, and felt my aunt should have vanished. I doubt if he even noticed that he had been sent to Coventry.

My aunt had arrived, on the day Paddy's pups were born, with her pedigree Airedale bitch, that was to be the source of wonderful pups. But one day a door was opened (and I was wrongly suspected of getting my own back because of Paddy, but it didn't enter my head and I doubt if I knew about seasons, being only ten) and Tinker mated with the town scruff.

She overdid her maternity and produced thirteen unwanted crossbred pups. I don't know what happened to the other twelve, but one day a small pup arrived for us. We named him Turk; he grew up to look like an Airedale but as he had been a cross, he hadn't had his tail docked. We never had the heart to have it done and he remained unique; a long-tailed Airedale with all the other Airedale characteristics.

He was a fantastic dog, enduring the vagaries of children who loved him too much, and I pretended he was entirely my dog, as mostly I took him out. For eight years I rarely went anywhere, except to school, unless I had the dog by my side.

We lived for some of that time in a vast old house with servants' quarters; a lovely house from our point of view, but a nightmare for my mother to run. It had front stairs and back stairs and a green baize door and two bathrooms, one of which was antiquated and bitterly cold, with an immense old bath with curly legs, and acres of chilly floor, and howling gales.

Part of the garden was wild, a wood separating the property from the new Rochester Bypass. Here I could lose myself for hours on end, sitting in a tree, with a book in my hand and Turk lying at the foot of the tree. Later, when I came to write the Paddy Joe books, Paddy Joe spent much of his time as I did, hidden from adults, aware of the wild life around him, and the dog below him, waiting patiently till he should decide to become active again. There was wild life in plenty in our wood then.

We lived in this particular house for only a few years, as war broke out soon after we had moved. In 1942 a German landmine demolished it completely. Luckily for the family I had just started at London University, which was evacuated to Bangor, North Wales, and they had followed me, as all of us went to school at Dartford, which had become a prohibited area. Both the boys' Grammar School which my brother attended, and the girls' school which my sisters went to, were closed.

My father worked for the BBC, in the advertising department, so that his work could be done quite easily anywhere in the country. So he moved the family to Bangor, where my brother and sisters could continue their schooling properly, instead of having papers set to work through during weeks spent at home. He rented a furnished house in Deiniol Road, and I left the hostel and joined the family.

Once more Turk became a major part of my life. I was nineteen and my twin brother and sister were fifteen; my younger sister was only twelve. We lived totally different lives. School continued long after College terms ended, and I was very much alone, as my friends worked in the vacations, but my father considered it improper for students to work. The long holidays were to catch up on reading, to make sure of essentials in each subject, and not for any other purpose.

But it is impossible to work for more than eight hours a day at books, even with the best of intentions, so that there were long summer evenings when I had nothing at all to do. Wartime Bangor, like most other cities, was devoid of entertainment, and television was not for the masses, even if it went on during the war. I simply can't remember and we didn't have a set.

I walked, mostly over Bangor mountain, with Turk. One bright day I watched a heron swept away in the rapids, both wings and legs broken. A fox? I never knew and I

13

dared not attempt the steep climb down to the water, or brave that savage desperate beak.

I walked endlessly, the dog happily by my side, watching, listening, observing. His nose told him of things I had not seen; his muzzle nudged my knee, warning me of hares and rabbits, stoats and farm animals. I spent long hours out of doors, guiltily, feeling I should be with the ATS or the WRENS, or driving an ambulance, as the world was bombing itself to blazes, and the boys I knew went away to fight.

Some of them never came back.

We were in limbo, waiting for time to pass; for the war to end; for life to begin again.

I gained a degree; and came to Manchester to work for ICI. No dog, but other people had dogs; friends' landladies had dogs; friends had dogs; and when I went home there was Turk to greet me.

Marriage came, and the end of the war and all the problems of ration books and no furniture; of babies and never enough clothing coupons; of restricted food, and trying to cope.

Turk died, and was succeeded by Thor, who was a bull terrier; I never took to him. I didn't live at home any longer, and he didn't know us well; he wasn't a particularly amiable dog and he was a doughty fighter, yet my mother had a very soft spot for him.

No dogs, Kenneth said. They don't go with our life style.

I supposed they didn't, so we bought Kym, Siamese, noisy, vocal, obstreperous, as much of a character as any dog.

He came with us all over the country and in between travels I borrowed dogs. Bramah and Brock in Ireland; dogs galore in England, culminating in Brandy, a Labrador who was so easy to teach that it felt like cheating to train him. He taught himself.

Kym developed cancer and was put to sleep in my arms one bleak day in April 1971.

By now our vet knew me well; knew my opinions on animals; knew how I hated cruelty; knew that our son was studying to be a vet; knew that I wanted a dog more than anything else on earth. Offer me diamonds or a pup and I'd choose the pup. What can you *do* with a diamond for goodness sake?

Kym had gone and the house was dead. Nothing moved. Anne went back to Sheffield. Kenneth went, for the next few days, to Germany. Andrew lived at home, but was out all day. Nick was away in Glasgow, at Bearsden, at the veterinary college.

Kenneth normally disappeared at seven-thirty in the morning; Andrew left just before eight. Kenneth often travelled abroad, leaving me for days and nights at a time. It's no fun at all being an executive's wife. You don't dare make arrangements as you can rarely keep them; a wedding anniversary? He's in Moscow, so you celebrate alone; a silver wedding for a friend; either you say No or ring up at the last minute to say, 'Sorry, can I come alone? He's flown to Washington at a moment's notice.'

A special supper, and back he comes to pack his case and fly off on the night plane to heaven knows where, leaving you high and dry, eating the meal alone once more.

On the only occasion on which Scout and Guide camp coincided and we were to be on our own, without the children, for the first time for nearly sixteen years, we made splendid plans; out to a meal every night; to the theatre; out on the spur of the moment without having to find out what everyone else was doing; no parents' night or speech days to attend; total freedom and absolute bliss.

I went out and bought a new dress, and had my hair done, and as I got in the phone rang.

'I've got unexpected American visitors; I'm out to dinner all week.'

I spent the rest of my week having delightful meals on my own—eggs.

But at least I had Kym for company and he often made me laugh. Without him, I was going to rattle around in an empty house pointlessly; without any sort of savour.

Meanwhile, how did I fill my leisure time? I was tied to home by the family; I did a number of outside reporting articles, but freelancing is dicey; you may or may not sell and rarely get commissioned; and I didn't feel that suburban life had anything to offer. All my friends had gone back to work. Research is too demanding for the mother of a family. It's a job that must come first.

I rang the vet.

'Do you know where there's a litter of Siamese kittens?' I asked.

'No. But I know where there's a litter of Golden Retriever pups. So far as I know they have sound temperaments and there are champions in their ancestry. Why don't you get that dog you've always hankered for?'

'Could I offer it much of a life?' I asked, thinking of country walks and large acres, and a place where a dog could run free. We had nowhere like that.

'If you don't take one, someone else will; it will have as good a home with you as anywhere in this area,' the tempter said, at the other end of the line.

I thought. I hadn't considered a dog, but the need for a dog had become greater over the years. I hated being without one. Brandy was becoming much too fond of me and I of him, and that wasn't fair to his owners. I would have to stop walking him soon.

I couldn't take a dog on Kenneth's boat. But I loathed the boat anyway, and my absence would be no loss as I spent my time curled up on the bunk, wishing the days away, marking them off on a private calendar, bored to screaming point, and hating every moment. If I had a dog I could spend my time in the country, could walk, could explore, could train him perhaps for field trials, especially if he were a retriever. My favourite breed.

16

No more listening to weather forecasts at 2 a.m. and 6 a.m. and finding out too late that you were in the only area that had an unforecasted gale; no more feeling sick for days on end, or bouncing at the mercy of wind and tide.

I thought of the goldies I knew; of Sam and of Dinah; of Della and Jason; of Henry and Jasper. All steady, sensible dogs with a sense of humour. Sam's is kinked. He likes to dig in the snow but only when women pass who are wearing thin nylon stockings. It doesn't work if they wear slacks. He waits for the critical moment, and enjoys the resultant noise. His owner pretends he isn't hers.

Beautiful Sam, whom I first met as a pup; he loved shoes and took the buckles off mine in two swift sorties; Ed, who is my agent, was highly embarrassed and stuck them back on for me. Ed is semi-retired now, with plenty of time for Sam, who has his own ideas about a number of things. Pat, Ed's daughter, deals with my writing complications these days. She owns Sam.

Sam loved to make mountains of shoes, so I bought him a squeaky shoe for a joke. I packed it, and sent it by post. The next time I met him, Sam took one sniff at me and ran off, puzzling his mistress very much.

'That's absurd,' Pat said. 'He must have recognised you.'

But it was nearly eighteen months since I'd last seen Sam. I knew he had forgotten and had gone off on some more important ploy.

A few minutes later he came pelting back, carrying in his mouth the squeaky shoe I had given him. He hadn't played with it for months. No one knew where it had been; no one had seen it for weeks. Yet Sam had taken one sniff at me and recognised the scent that had been on the toy I had wrapped for him and posted; and had brought it to show me, and now we had a great reunion, with Sam proudly carrying his shoe, groaning, tail waving, greeting me as if he had been waiting all this time for me and for no one else.

I remembered that and thought of a retriever pup of my own.

And I knew that I had no choice at all.

No matter what the family said, I would buy my Golden Retriever.

I didn't tell anyone my plan. They would try to talk me out of it and I didn't intend to spend any more time without a dog. I remembered telling my teachers I was going to breed dogs. That wouldn't come yet, but maybe later I would buy a bitch.

I booked an appointment next day, to see the pups.

Chapter 2

They were older than I expected; not tiny pups, just weaned, about to leave the mother, but aged, the breeder said, thirteen weeks, almost adolescent, big, bumbling, delightful. There were three. I couldn't make up my mind, but friends who breed dogs had said firmly, 'Leave it to the breeder; that way, you'll be given a pup that will suit you. People are surprisingly perceptive.'

The breeder picked one up.

'This is the one I'd choose of the three.'

I wanted, later, to take up Obedience. I wanted my dog for a number of reasons. Writing is a lonely profession; long hours dedicated to people in Cloud Cuckoo Land, people who sometimes become more real than your friends; who dominate your life. Their problems become yours; it's necessary to know every character better than you know yourself; know why they do things, what makes them tick. The man who has never moved from his own village is going to be very different in outlook from the man who has spent ten years in jungle warfare; or the man who spends his life climbing mountains; or the man whose whole existence is dominated by his racing greyhound.

My dog was to help me get away from my desk; for exercise and fresh air; he was for companionship; and because both Andrew and Kenneth work hard and are very tired by evening, he had to be a fairly sensible animal, not a bubbling loon, for ever moving restlessly about the room.

And he would have to be trained.

Retrievers were perfect as they need forty minutes' exercise a day and are steady sensible dogs.

I knew that; the books said that and this one seemed steady and sensible, a sober little fellow, fluffy with puppy fur, with big sad eyes and a tail that didn't even pretend to wag, but then he didn't know me. I lifted him. He was most remarkably heavy.

'They are very mature pups,' the breeder said.

I had my dog.

Steady, sober, sensible.

The gods that laugh at humans were watching us; someone had to be joking.

I thought of calling him Jason, the golden dog, after Jason of the Golden Fleece, but every second yellow or golden dog is Jason, so I decided instead to name him Janus, after the god who guarded gates and doors and gave his name to January, at the doorway of the year, and the janitors who watch over buildings. Also I had named a book 'Jason', which Disney are now filming and it would be better to choose a different name. My fictional Jason had been a Labrador; Janus was a retriever.

I took him straight out of the car and put him on the lawn, where he promptly produced the most horrible mess that any pup ever made. I took my pup to the vet straight away.

He had enteritis; he had tonsillitis; you couldn't see down his throat for the immense red swellings; he also had a broken tail, half healed, broken about three weeks before. No wonder it didn't wag. No wonder he was so sober.

'Take him back,' the vet said.

I looked at the pup, watching me with those enormous eyes. He had a temperature, and his home had been a draughty wooden shed. And I had a sudden conviction that could never be proved that he had already been sold once and returned and this was his second time round.

What would happen if he did go back?

'I'll keep him,' I said.

I knew I was being a fool. I knew enough about dogs to know that, to get the best results you must take your puppy at between seven and eight weeks old. That is the age at which socialisation starts, and during the next few weeks the dog-human bond is formed. The pups learn most between six and sixteen weeks of age. What they learn is there for life, and if they are not given human companionship then, the owner loses out.

I knew that this pup had already learned bad habits; maybe very bad habits. He had reached an age at which he should have been familiar with the world, but he had never seen it. No one had given him a name; or taught him to come; or even taught him that humans meant pleasure, meant fun, meant walks, and all the other things that dogs love.

No human had played with him.

He had his kennel mates and had played dog games; rough dog games without anyone to chide, or stop the fights that sometimes developed. The vet looked at me, knowing as well as I did that I was taking on an awful lot, and was in for a tough time.

How tough, I didn't realise. Just as I had with our Siamese Kym, a cat's lifetime before, I ignored my own common sense and the vet's warnings. The pup was too ill to have his preventive inoculations. He wouldn't be able to go out into the big wide world for weeks yet; and it was soon very obvious that he had learned not to trust people.

He trusted me. I had picked him up, fussed him, and praised him. He watched everything I did, followed me like a forlorn little shadow. On the second day, his inside proved too upset for him to take even a short journey. I rang and asked the vet to call.

21

An agitated pup resisted every movement made towards him until I held him and reassured him, soothing him, trying to get through into his frightened little brain that this was safety; no one was going to hurt him. It was all for his own good.

I went out of the room to wash the thermometer, and when I returned the vet commented that he had never seen a puppy attach itself so fast to an owner. The pup had run to the door, watching for my return.

He greeted me as if I had been away for weeks.

That was one good sign. It meant that the months to come would be that much easier, as the pup regarded me already as his; and he might not have attached at all but remained one of those aloof and unrewarding dogs that never has any sort of affection for those with whom he lives.

He had walked out into unfamiliar surroundings that he didn't like but I had comforted him and soothed him, and talked softly to him. I was the one stable element in this new life, and he wasn't going to let me out of his sight, not for one minute. He cried whenever he was left.

He felt ill and he was desperately forlorn.

He was plunged into an alarming world; a world so full of new sights and sounds and strangeness that he was terrified.

I hadn't told either Kenneth or Andrew about the pup. They weren't going to have the chance to talk me out of it; I spent so much time entirely alone. Neither was exactly pleased to find Kym ousted by a sick puppy that loathed them both on sight and rushed to me for protection from these towering loud-voiced men whose voices held disapproval. Even the smallest puppy is sensitive to atmosphere and knows who likes him and who doesn't.

'What on earth did you get *that* for?'

I never did really manage to explain to the family just why I'd bought a dog. Dogs had been so much part of my life that it seemed almost a crime to live without one any longer. I would have liked a farm, and stables; but failing that, I could have a pup. The family had no idea where I spent my afternoon. They talked. I listened, and kept my own counsel.

I made plans.

I have now learned better.

That continued to be a problem. We were back to our old routine, and the vet grew to know Janus as well as he had known Kym. Glucose and water was the pup's main diet; medicine daily. House training was complicated by diarrhoea. Luckily he was a biddable little animal; not so little now, and growing rapidly, in spite of all his troubles. He rarely wagged his tail; he was careful of it too, going cautiously past furniture, holding it away from people, always aware of it, probably because it hurt. It had two almost healed breaks, about an inch apart. It is still kinked, bent almost in two at right angles, though he has learned to hold it so cleverly that the long plumes hide the odd shape.

We never did discover how it got broken. The kennels denied it.

Training a pup is a matter of patience and observation. He will empty as soon as he wakes; immediately after he is fed; and in between as well. Janus was easy to catch as he ran round in frantic circles sniffing the ground when he needed to go outside and I picked him up and whipped him out fast, and praised him extravagantly when he had performed in the proper places.

'Good dog. What a lovely boy. What a *clever* pup.'

It's the only way your dog knows that he is right; a silent approval doesn't work, nor does ignoring him; nor taking him for granted; he just has to be taught and your voice is the one thing that helps him to learn fast. Dogs love hammy acting, so if an owner overdoes the praise for a pup, with lots of happy chat, that pup will learn far quicker than a pup in a household that feels it is silly to talk to a dog.

A good cowman sings to his cows as he milks them; soft and soothing, and the milk comes fast. Swear and fuss, and the cows will give a far lower yield. I once travelled between two Scottish islands on a cargo boat, with a bull chained firmly in a cage, while the farmer, a dour elderly Scotsman, sang hymns to the animal all the way over the sea, keeping him quiet and biddable, and free from fear. The human voice has great power if only we learn how to use it properly.

The tonsils went down, very slowly. Janus began to play with me, and to accept Kenneth and Andrew, and to go to Dorothy who typed for me part time and coped with post and shopping, but he still had to be kept indoors, or in our garden, as he wasn't well enough for those all-important injections. And I wasn't risking distemper or hardpad; I had known too many pups die from that, or end up with fits for life. Any immunity he had inherited from his mother had long since disappeared. He was well over five months old.

I was having trouble with his feeding. I kept, rigidly, to the diet sheet that the breeder had given me, and used the meat I had bought with him. But nothing suited him, and worse, he never ate up. He ran to his plate, took a few nibbles and ran off to play. It was an idiotic way for a pup to behave. Most of them eat as if this was the last meal they would see; and hunt around after the plate is clean.

Not Janus.

After his few quick bites, he hunted for something to carry. Anything, whether suitable or unsuitable. He liked to root in the dirty linen box and carry odd socks about, convinced this is what retrievers were for. But eat a proper meal ... not he.

In desperation I rang the breeder. With so many pups at a time, around forty, the food was put out in the morning

24

and left down all day. They fed as they liked, a bit now and a bit then and it didn't matter in the least so long as they got the food.

Maybe it doesn't matter; quite a lot of big kennels do feed that way, but pups empty after feeding and non-stop clean-up isn't practicable in a house; nor is taking the puppy out after every three or four nibbles. He would just have to relearn new ways. I didn't want a kennel-kept dog.

The breeders I know personally, as friends, *don't* feed that way; each pup is fed individually. Or some will take twice as much as they need and others will not get enough. Nor do they breed more than one or at most two litters at a time.

When the vet came to give yet another injection I asked him how I could retrain the pup.

There was only one way. Starve him for twenty-four hours, and then give him a tiny meal. The pup was so thin that this sounded drastic, but he wasn't getting enough anyway, as he just wasn't interested in food. He didn't even bother when he had to go without. But he *was* hungry after a day and a night without food, and the first tiny meal he had he ate properly, and looked for more.

At last he was on to a proper diet and four meals a day.

He was still producing the most horrible messes and they most certainly weren't normal. If I went out, or away for a day Dorothy left me notes on my desk, as she went home at two.

'Janus *did*. In the proper place. Looked a bit better than usual.'

Or else,

'Janus did. Ugh!'

Medicine was a daily routine. It helped, but not much. He had a drug which slowed his digestion down. He was excessively excitable, a little wild dog in every way, and extremely difficult to control. We had to be very firm.

He learned to 'sit' for his meals. He learned to lie quietly when I wrote. He learned not to snap at his food. I put it down for him, and then moved it away and made him wait a second time for it until he learned to stay quietly while I got it ready.

He learned that growls were not acceptable. I shook him gently if he growled at me. He learned to give me his bone; I buy treated marrow bones from the pet shop, which are almost indestructible, and last for months. I don't like ordinary bones for dogs; they can cause trouble. A dog with a dodgy digestion needed something to teeth on, but not anything that might make matters worse.

I seemed to spend an awful lot of time thinking about the dog.

I looked at the vet bills. They came to far more than his food and I began to feel guilty; I *had* bought myself a pup; an expensive little headache, that was far from fit, that was far from steady and sober, that was very hard to train. Competition obedience would be out of the question. It was going to be all I could do to train him for normal living, let alone anything else, and I began to think I would have to have him put down and start again.

And if he were put down Kenneth and Andrew would say 'I told you so. No more dogs.' Certainly no more pedigree dogs. They were saying I should have got myself a tough mongrel. But no mongrel is better than its parents.

I wanted a Golden Retriever. I still wanted one, but next time round I would ask a lot more questions before I bought; would study litters and the pups that came from them; would find other buyers, and see if they had had trouble too. It was partly my own fault, but I had never expected this kind of trouble, as I had not yet realised that far too many pups were bred just for the pet market. You can't breed quality in quantity.

The decision would have been easier to make if life had been all illness but it wasn't. When Janus and I were alone, quite alone, he was a different pup. He was relaxed, merry, playful, full of energy, delighting in absurd games with me. He enjoyed learning and learned fast, and he was inventive.

He found his own games, playing endlessly with a ball, or teasing a piece of rope, shaking it to 'kill' it, chasing his tail in a wild circle until he fell over and lay on his back, his paw in his mouth, his ears flopping off his head, his eyes glinting, curious to see how I was taking this absurd attitude. He loved to lie on his back when we were alone, often against the front door, legs in the air, expression totally blissful, or come and lie against my shoe, watching me, waiting hopefully for something to happen, so that we could play again. He loved to 'bicycle', energetic, and idiotic, grinning.

He adored playing ball, especially with a big football that he could butt back to me. He adored cheese, and barked for it; he had begun to endear himself to Kenneth, who, coming in tired, often flopped in the big chair, doing nothing. Within minutes Janus would be at his side, paw on his knee, eyes anxious.

'I'm here. Have you forgotten me?'

A stroke and a pat and he was away, dashing round the room in ecstasy, being a greyhound, full of energy and puppy merriment, chasing his tail again, so delighted to be noticed.

So how could I put him down?

But dear Heaven, the size of those vet bills and the knowledge that he might go on like this for ever; he showed no sign of improvement.

He began to lose his baby teeth and began to chew.

I don't like destructive dogs, so Janus had to learn. He had to realise, once and for all time, that tearing up our property just wasn't on. So in the afternoons, as we couldn't go out yet, after Dorothy had gone, we had a puppy teach-in.

I strewed the floor with everything chewable I could

think of. Shoes, handbag, letters, books, papers, articles typed in manuscript, handkerchiefs. Among this debris I put his bone and his ball and his dog pull; and his squeaky red rat, a Christmas present from Sam's owner. He adored that rat.

Whenever he touched anything of mine I said *No*, and took it away from him, substituting a toy of his own, and a little romp to show that that was something he *could* have. It became a well loved game. He would nose something of mine and look at me, waiting for a reaction; *No*; and at once he'd pick up his own property with an air of achievement and come for approval. Clever boy! Within a month, he would hunt out his own possessions and leave mine alone. I bought a teak box on castors, with a table top and his toys were kept in here. When he felt like a game he opened it and took out whatever he wanted; often a ball that he brought to me and chucked at me. Come on for goodness sake; you've typed long enough; let's have fun.

If he did do wrong, he was shaken. Taken by the throat and given a small reprimanding shake; later, as he grew, the shakes were harder. I don't like smacking dogs; but a shake upsets their dignity. Mum shakes her bad pups; they hate it, and it's a much better way of keeping control and showing who is Boss, as if you aren't Boss, your dog will be; he is a pack animal and he likes to lead the pack. He has to learn his place.

Shaking is useful for a pup that is puddling indoors. It's very little use punishing him half an hour after the act; he can't think why, as his memory is such that he forgets instantly what he has done. Punish him and he may think he has been punished for coming to you, and refuse to come next time. Catch him in the act and shake him and put him out and praise him when he's done right, and you get results. I personally think it is quite unspeakable to rub a small animal's nose in a mess, whether it is a puppy or a kitten or an older dog. All that it teaches it is that you

28

have horrible and unpredictable habits. It doesn't teach it that messes are unacceptable.

Pups don't foul their own nests. They just have to learn that the *whole house is the nest* and not only the box they sleep in, and sometimes they fail to learn because the human doesn't know how to teach. I found it necessary to review everything I did with the pup, all the time. Some mistakes and faults were of my own making.

It is easy to teach a tiny pup to come to you. But Janus wasn't a tiny pup; he had had sixteen weeks at least in which to learn disobedience; no one had given him a name or called him; no one had taught him it was unacceptable to bark and whine whenever he felt like it; no one had taught him that he must do as he was told. It didn't matter, in a kennel, what he did, or where he did it; he had been confined in a small space, and left to his own devices.

Teaching Janus to 'come' proved a major headache. Fine, on the lead. He couldn't *not* come, but he had already learned that if he ran away fast enough no one could catch him.

And besides that, he wanted to be *my* Boss. He didn't like *being* bossed. And one way he could defy me was by not coming. In the end both Dorothy and I learned it was useless calling him; it only taught him that his name had no significance whatever, but he loved playing with a rag, playing a violent game of tug of war, grumbling away in a chatty voice as he pulled. So when we wanted him we shook a cloth, and he came fast, eager to play.

By now he was having a few more good days. He played racing, tearing round the garden, ears flying, tail tucked under his legs, going fast. He loved chasing swallows. They seemed to enjoy it too, and teased him. It was the only time he moved well. He had the oddest gait, moving at each step as if his back were dislocated, rolling his hips. The vet had looked at this suspiciously, and mentioned possible trouble, but as he was able to run, and seemed to have no discomfort at all when he walked, I didn't take much notice of it. The veterinary term meant nothing.

If he continued fit, we could get him inoculated and he would be able to come out with me. I looked forward to going out and about. He came in the car, but he couldn't yet mix. I also planned to take him to a dog club as there was one advertised in the vet's waiting room. I rang the Head Trainer and discovered it was on Monday nights at the Parish Hall in Wood's Lane, Cheadle Hulme. Jill would be pleased to see us.

Neither she nor I knew what we were in for.

Janus was no longer a meek little dog, barely wagging his tail. He had grown to enormous proportions, seeming far too large for a five-month-old pup. He was losing his puppy coat; was, when he was well, boisterous and enthusiastic and he now flagged his tail, frequently, noisily, thumping it against the furniture, greeting us gleefully. And he brought us presents.

Janus's presents were likely to be almost anything; from the bath brush or the loofah to a sock someone had left on the bathroom floor; or his blanket, which he preferred (and still does) in a huddle in the middle of the living-room floor. As soon as the room is clean and tidy he becomes anxious; it's not natural. His belongings accumulate rapidly, producing a much more relaxed atmosphere where a dog can feel at home.

His most treasured object is a filthy ancient scarlet sock, relic of someone's football days, which he unearths from unlikely hiding places, and offers to our friends. They are rarely enchanted.

One night, Kenneth and I went to the pictures. It was a memorable occasion, one which we not only planned but which actually came off, as we both wanted to see *Butch Cassidy and the Sundance Kid*. For once I didn't have to go with a friend or not at all, as I don't enjoy the cinema by myself.

We came home late, expecting Janus to be at the door with a present for us.

He wasn't.

Instead there was a noise that sounded as if we had rather mad burglars in the house. Crash. Bang. Thump.

I switched on the dining-room light.

We hadn't left one single portable object about. The only thing that would move was our very large hearth rug. Janus held the corner firmly in his mouth and was navigating precariously round the rest of it, trying not to tread on it when it became embarrassingly stationary; dragging it, tail wagging furiously, making whimpering, groaning, greeting noises, agonised with pleasure and the desire to meet us properly, as all retrievers must, with a 'pheasant' in his mouth. He banged into things; he tripped. But by now I knew my pup.

Janus is a soldier, and on he goes, never mind the difficulties. He has to achieve. He reached us, his dignity hurt because we were laughing at his efforts and we had to fuss him and reassure him and find something smaller for him to carry while we restored the rug to its place.

He has never outgrown the need to bring a gift when I get up, or come home; the desire to fetch something, anything; the instinct bred in him to find game in the field shouting for an outlet. Heredity is sometimes a frightening thing. It cannot be denied.

It was about now that he also developed a genius for misunderstanding. If I were busy, or we had friends, and the puppy was boisterous and obtrusive, (he is a born show-off) I would say 'bed'. Very obediently off he would go, and I would settle, knowing that he was safely in his box.

Not Janus.

That penny never did drop till I took him firmly in hand. His idea of 'bed' was to bring his blanket, pile it into a messy muddle at my feet, and with a deep sigh and a reproachful look settle on it and proceed to try and stare me out.

He was settled quietly, doing no harm, so I left him to it. In time he learned that he didn't have to have his blanket in order to lie down and be good; he could do it quite well without, safely by my feet.

Janus now knew he was *mine*.

And then I heard of a litter of Siamese kittens. I missed Kym; at home, as a child, we had always had cats and dogs. In my opinion, they belong together. I had the pup; if I bought a kitten they would grow up together and play together, and as they weren't likely to die at the same time I would never again have that awful gap or the need to buy an animal in a hurry, which is never wise.

I went to see the kittens.

Chapter 3

There were five kittens; three seal points and two blue points, as the little seal point queen had been mated to a blue point stud cat, a very lordly cat, High Peak Peveril. The seal points were sold, but not the blue. The two blue point kittens sat side by side, inscrutable, watching me. Wouldn't it be a pity to separate them?

I hadn't considered buying two kittens. Just one, as a companion for Janus. But Janus and I would travel; and a little cat left alone at home would be more forlorn than Kym, who had never known a companion in the house, other than his human family.

The kittens were exquisite, and so tiny after my huge pup. They sat there, delicate grey on masks and tails and ears, immaculate creamy coats, vivid blue eyes, watching me. I was glad there wasn't a seal point available. There would always be comparisons and no other cat could measure up to Kym. The blue would be different. I wouldn't be tempted to compare. Common sense said it would be ridiculous to take two.

I picked up the little tom. He snuggled against me, purring, watching me, accepting me, sniffing at my hair and nose, and then at my clothes, smelling dog. His sister jumped up too, crowding him, purring in her turn, pushing her minute body against my hand, tail arched in the air, confident of a welcome.

They sat on my knee, side by side, staring at me. The little female cuddled against her brother, put her paws round his neck and washed his ears.

I was sunk.

Home they came, complete with their pedigree. Numenor Elrond and Numenor Celeborn, named after the fairy king and queen in the *Lord of the Rings*. Their breeder taught English. Tolkien is one of my favourite authors; they were destined for me. I salved my nagging conscience, especially as once more I had kept my intentions dark. The kittens, like Janus, would be a *fait accompli*; no arguments no one trying to put me off, saying that Kym could never be supplanted. Life as lived in a suburb had little to offer; without the animals to make me laugh, it had even less. Escape in the afternoons to farms and kennels was too temporary. I had to return, to bricklined streets, and dirty pavements, and a garden that gave me a lot of pleasure but very little scope.

One day we would pack up and find a cottage in the country.

But one day was a long way off, then.

I couldn't shout Elrond and Celeborn when I wanted the kittens; and Ellie and Cellie, or El and Cel both sounded daft, so we kept their beautiful names for best, pedigree names for state occasions, and named them Chia and Casey, after two of my books, written long before these mites had been dreamed of.

They are characters in their own way, but nothing like Kym. Timid Chia, gentle and confiding, lives most of her life in cupboards, wary of visitors, honouring only those who *really* like cats with her presence. She knows who professes to like them; and who is genuine. I now know too which of my friends tolerates cats, and which is besotted. Surprising, more men than women are attracted to cats. Or maybe Chia prefers men.

Casey is slant-eyed and wicked, bullying his sister, lying

34

in wait on the stairs to see who is there, and coming, deliberately, showing off his elegance, but biting anyone who dares to try to lift him against his will. Those who know him wait for him to favour them; they try to force him on to a lap.

All my cats have learned that if I pat my knee, it means 'OK, come up'. They sit at my feet neatly contained, tails curled round lean bodies, watching until I notice them and give the necessary invitation. Kym rarely waited for it, though if he felt like honouring me, he would come when I patted at times; these two wait to be asked, unless I happen to be in the direct route to somewhere they want to go, and then they walk across me, using me as a right of way.

Kym also used me as his bathroom, washing himself thoroughly on my knee—but Chia and Casey bath each other, curled up tightly together in a chair, meticulous in their daily grooming.

They came into the house where the pup ruled supreme, and there was trouble. They moved like squirrels, up and up and up, swearing and hissing like tiny demons, while he sat beneath them, mouth open, laughing at them, trying to entice them to come down and play.

But play with Janus might have been lethal. I hadn't realised the immense difference in size. The dog had stayed in the car while I inspected the cats.

I have never used cat baskets; Kym hated the dark. I have a wire veterinary cage in which the kittens had travelled, as two would have to be shut up safely when they came away; Kym only came when all of us were in the car; he wore a collar and lead, like a dog, and sat on a lap. Since the family grew up and I had my own car, more often than not I travelled alone.

I put the kittens inside the cage and put it down on the floor.

Janus sniffed at it, intrigued. The kittens swore and batted at his face with angry paws. He thought it very funny. He wagged his tail and sniffed again. He sat, watching them.

After a few minutes they settled into compact little balls and watched him, realising that he couldn't reach them. They were safe.

I settled back in my chair, to watch in my turn.

Janus went to find a present. He brought them his beloved red squeaky rat and chucked it at the cage. It fell beside it. The kittens watched, unmoving. No response. He found his ball and tried that. Four unwinking eyes stared at him.

He brought his rope twist and tried to 'kill' it, shaking it furiously, tossing it and catching it and then shaking it again. It hit the edge of the cage with a resounding thwack, and I realised that this toy would have to go. A kitten might be blinded if he shook it too close to those tiny heads. He was a very strong pup.

I put the cage on the table and started a Janus 'teach in' while the kittens watched, fascinated, coming to the edge of the cage to see better. They were intensely curious and so long as the dog couldn't get at them, seemed quite unmoved by his presence. Their fluffed fur was sleek, and they had stopped swearing.

It was 'taking food from my hand' sessions, using a small dog biscuit, as Janus was now a hungry pup, and he tended to snatch at his food. 'Take it nicely. Don't snatch.' A tap on the nose and the biscuit was withdrawn and we started again. The idea came at last, as I put the biscuit to his lips, closing my hand over them so that he touched me softly, gently, and took the food and ate it. A second time, and a third, and we were getting the message across.

Now, if he gets over enthusiastic, a 'Gently' is enough to remind him to behave himself and not snap. It's all too easy to get an accidental bite that way.

The kittens stayed in my study to begin with and whenever they came out to meet the dog they were put safely inside the cage.

After a week I began to let them free, so long as I was there. The kittens lived, for months, on the backs of chairs or on the top of the table, out of the way of those enormous paws, occasionally trying to catch the dog's tail as he ran by. He nosed them, and licked them, if he could catch them. Often I found a soaked kit, frantically trying to dry itself off, with an air of total disgust, presumably hating the taste of dog saliva.

They decided their minute water bowl was too absurd, and drank instead from Janus's vast bowl, big enough to bath them in. Sighing deeply, he drank from theirs, which doubled as a feeding bowl, but it just wasn't the same. The cats now do deign to use their small bowl, but Janus likes it too.

Meals were hilarious, as I prepared an enormous bowl of meal and meat and medicine for Janus and two teaspoonsful each of food for the cats, on saucers. If I wasn't careful the dog put his paws on the table, stretched out his neck and demolished the cats' meal in two swift licks. Anguished wails told me that they had lost their dinner yet again.

Like Kym, like Janus, many of their first meals were eaten, not from a saucer, but from my cupped hand. The smell of an owner, coupled with the smell of food quickly teaches who is the source of the main comforts of their lives, and establishes trust, which is the only basis on which an animal/human relationship can survive; perhaps trust works with humans too, if only we had the chance more often.

When the kittens ventured on to the floor, I put Janus on his lead. One stamp of those huge clumsy paws could have meant a broken back. He reminded me of the Tenniel drawing of the puppy looking down on Alice in the rabbit hole; a vast head and a tiny girl reduced by magic to kitten dimensions. The kits were little bigger than his two floppy ears, and he seemed to have doubled in size, compared with them, almost overnight.

We were still having tummy trouble. I took the kittens to the vet for inspection; they had already had their injections, before the breeder sold them. They were both thoroughly healthy. Janus came in too for another injection. Some days were impossible. It was incredible that a pup should have so much waste inside him, and yet be lively and active. Nobody could understand it. I had hoped that we could leave off the pills which slowed his digestion down, but they and his vitamin pills seemed to be all that he *was* digesting; he was so thin, I was ashamed of him. Every rib showed. His coat was harsh, and if his tummy was really bad, he was forlorn and apathetic and the colic was painful and he cried.

But the attacks were now more widely spaced.

He had his first protective inoculation and I began to get him more used to the car. He didn't like it much. The engine noises worried him and so did the movement, and he salivated heavily, which made me wonder if, on a long journey, he might well be sick. Pat's Sam was car sick, and I knew how much trouble she had when travelling. I didn't want that.

I sat in the car in the garage, door open, while the pup nosed around. He came to me, and climbed in of his own accord. He curled up at my feet, that being where a dog did go, so I moved from the driver's seat to the passenger seat, to teach him to curl up there, and not among the pedals. I put his blanket there, just to show him that this was yet another place where a dog could lie.

By the end of the week it was quite natural for him to curl up on his blanket in the well in front of the passenger seat while I sat and read, in the driver's seat. I was rather glad the garage had no windows that gave on to the road, as it was an odd place to read, and most town people and some dog owners don't understand the needs of dogs. A little trouble taken in the early days can save so much later on, and it didn't really matter whether I corrected manuscripts in my car or in my study. I did wait till Dorothy had gone; I was already sure that she thought I was more than ordinarily batty.

So I didn't tell her I corrected most of her work sitting in the car in the garage all afternoon while the dog slept beside me, on the floor.

Soon the car was familiar territory, and now I opened the garage doors, and backed out into the drive. Movement and the engine noise was disturbing and Janus wasn't so sure, but I stopped the engine, fed him with a biscuit, and reassured him. It's OK. Cars do that.

Round the block; round two blocks; to the vet, this time with me driving, and Janus by himself on the floor, instead of with someone else, and me holding on to the pup. And then began the longer journeys, until now he is a veteran traveller, by train, by taxi, by car, lying quite still while the car is moving, knowing he mustn't bumble about, as I don't like my mirror blocked by a fretful dog wandering around. Some dogs are major pests when travelling because no one has ever thought of training them to be reasonable as passengers. Janus learned quickly to behave himself in the car.

I never leashed him; that can be dangerous. Dogs have caught their check chains round the handbrake and choked to death; one lovely little pup I knew, tied by his lead to the door handle, managed to climb on to the back of the car seat and slip, and hang himself. Mine only wear collars if they travel behind the dog guard in my car, where I know there is nothing whatever that can catch.

I took him across to the vet for his second injection.

At last we could go out. I had been practising with collar and lead in the garden, as many dogs hate collars and hate leads. First a ribbon round a puppy neck, getting him used to the feeling of some constriction, though not very much, and then a light soft cat collar, elasticated; and a string dangling from it; that is a toy to play with. Pick up the string and wave the big red squeaky rat and the pup runs towards it, quite unaware that he is under restraint, but coming to my side. He adored his rat so much that he still steals red squeaky rats if he comes across one. They are often used as decoys at the shows.

Later a lead, held lightly, and still the rubber rat to tease at and run after, and then a long game, good dog, wasn't that fun?

When I bought the pup, I had the garden fenced, all the way round; chain link fencing, supported by concrete posts, buried so that he couldn't dig his way out. There was a high gate, nearly seven feet high, bolts top and bottom and the dustbins were outside that, so that dustmen could never come into the garden by accident and let the pup free.

In spite of this, Janus wore a collar with his name tag on it (not his name, but ours; it never does to let a possible thief know what to call a dog). He was used to his collar. He was now used to the lead, and in the garden he walked by my side without fuss, beautifully under control. He knew how to sit and he knew 'stay', though he hated that, and wouldn't do it at all off lead.

I would take him for his first walk and then start at the training club.

I did not expect trouble of any kind. He was so good, in the garden, and he was used to walking beside me now, even though we had only done it round and round the lawn.

I looked forward immensely to taking him to the park; to getting him used to the world. It was high time he met other people and other dogs.

I put him on the lead and we started out.

He pulled like a steam train, bolting round the block, panic driven, racing in terror from the smells that surged up at him, diving against the wall, tail between his legs, panting at the top of his voice, as a car came by.

He was immensely strong.

I know now what I didn't know then.

He was much more than six months old; he was a full-grown, very powerful dog, that hadn't met anything early enough in life.

It was one hell of a walk.

Chapter 4

I must, during my life, have walked more than fifty dogs at various times, but I have never walked a dog like Janus. Neither before nor since.

A milk float came by, and we took off, almost faster than I could run. He was so strong I could barely hold him. I tripped, and went flat on my face, luckily with the lead round my wrist. Equally luckily, the dog was stopped and I wasn't badly hurt.

I looked at that break in his tail. I would like to know the truth, but we can only guess. Those who saw his reaction and know dogs guess the same way as I do.

He loathed the milk float, was terrified of the milkman, shivered at the sight of the crates and once when I accidentally clashed two milk bottles together as I brought them into the house, he bolted upstairs and hid under a bed and refused to come out for ages.

I carried him out to the float next time, with extreme difficulty. He struggled to get down and run.

The milkman was friendly and very pleasant, and upset by the dog's reaction; even more upset one Sunday when we were out walking, and he passed by, in his best clothes. I didn't recognise him. Janus did, and barked at him, frantic.

The milkman gave him cheese, tried to make friends;

gave him biscuits. We once even tried a ride in the float. We met the float daily, but nothing would allay the panic.

I told our vet, who commented that his Collie pup had been burnt on the ear, when only a few weeks old, by a spark that exploded from a coal fire. The dog is now nine, but he won't go into a room with a fire in it and if he hears a bang when he is out, he takes off, and races home.

Something had happened at a crucial age. I now had a choice. Either I owned a dog I left at home, and only took out in the car, or I taught him there was nothing to fear about traffic. There are two ways of doing that. One is by making the dog more afraid of you than of the traffic, but *I* can't do that; maybe it works much faster, but it goes against my own nature. It's a case of being cruel to be kind. Sometimes there is no other way, but I wanted to try the other way first, and if we did have to change to the tough way then someone better versed in the ways of teaching difficult dogs than I would have to do it for me.

I did it the slow way, which is the hard way.

Daily, we had a dog walk. First, return to the start and choose a time when it is quiet and no milk floats about, and round the block. Fine; nothing to panic about is there? No nasty noisy cars; no big lorries; no milk floats. Once there was a rainy day and two terrifying creatures came towards us; they had legs, like people, but instead of heads they had mushrooms over them.

They rustled, and then quite unnervingly, spoke to me.

Janus barked.

'They're only umbrellas.'

He didn't intend to like umbrellas either, so out came Kenneth's old holey one, and we played around it on the lawn; we put it up a little way, and Janus sniffed it; we put it all the way up and he backed off, suspicious, watching me to make sure it really *was* me; not some odd thing I had suddenly changed into in a moment. Humans do such

43

crazy things and none of them can make much sense to a dog.

A few weeks later he had a panic in the park. No reason at all that I could see. He sat, refusing to move, trembling. All I could see ahead of me was a man carrying a child against his shoulder. I glanced away and back again and in that quick moment saw what the dog was seeing.

You couldn't see the child's body, only his head, against his father's head. A man with two heads.

I called out to the man and he turned round.

'My dog won't pass you, may we come by now?'

He must have thought I was mad, but Janus looked at him and saw the child being held and eyed me sheepishly, apparently aware that he had made a mistake and not quite sure if I knew too what he had thought.

Meanwhile, we were still getting used to traffic. The park was OK; very few cars there and those go slowly, but main roads were another matter entirely. He would walk so long as I talked. 'Good lad. It's OK now. It can't hurt you; steady now, slowly, slowly, that's a good dog. Come on then.'

They weren't pleasurable walks; they were mini nightmares.

Side roads began to be less daunting and it was time to tackle the main roads. Out of Westfield into Highfield Road. Not too bad as the traffic, though fast moving, isn't continuous. And then into Turves Road which is a link between the A34 Manchester to Ringway Airport, Manchester to London, Stockport to London or to Motorway roads. Traffic all the time, moving fast and far too heavy for the width of the road, which wasn't built to take it.

Stroke and sit, and start again. Comfort and reassure. Down into Cheadle Hulme main street, across the Belisha crossing, up into Mellor Road, to take the short cut home into the comparative peace of Swann Lane and Hill Top and Upton Avenue.

Across the Belisha crossing? I had to be joking. There were those weird stripes on the road and the beacons that flashed at him; and then he went flat on the ground, trembling, all four paws glued, as an immense monster, belching smoke from its hind end, rattled thunderously towards him, jammed on its brakes with a whoosh of air, and a crash of its load that made my ears hurt, never mind the dog's.

I tried to lift him but he was too heavy.

I tried to coax him, but he was blind and deaf with terror.

I tried to drag him, but he wasn't having that. He pulled back.

The lorry driver watched me and then climbed down from his cab, picked up the dog effortlessly and carried him across. 'Bit scared,' he said, patting the dog. 'He'll get over it.'

It was the understatement of all time.

By now I really was wondering.

Trust came slowly, but it did come, and we had no more trouble there until one day a child ran out of the station, across the crossing, without looking, and a woman jammed on her brakes. The car behind failed to stop in time and crashed into the rear of her vehicle, with the noise of a thousand roaring devils.

We were only yards away and to make matters worse, the child, though unhurt, was badly frightened and screaming, and the occupants of the two cars appeared to be about to come to blows. It was useless even trying to cross. I retraced my steps, cursing to myself.

We were back to the beginning. He had only tolerated that crossing, which is very near the station, and a railway bridge across which mainline expresses frequently seemed to thunder just as we approached; cars hoot as they come down the hill. It is a 30 mile an hour zone, but few would guess that.

We had to face that crossing, or spend our lives in the

car. I decided to try in the evenings. Kenneth was often away, Andrew invariably out, and I might just as well walk then as earlier in the day. There was rarely any programme that attracted me overwhelmingly on television. I don't like being fed my entertainment; I prefer to make it for myself.

We walked every evening.

We stopped and watched the trains.

We sat by the bus stop at the traffic lights on Turves Road, Janus leaning against me, ears back, eyes anxious, body whipcord tense, tail tucked under his legs.

All the time I talked to him. 'Good boy. Good lad. Clever dog. It's OK. Not to worry. It won't hurt you.'

No use being angry. That wouldn't have helped.

No use remembering my other dogs, totally unafraid of traffic. We plodded on, day after day, with barely perceptible improvement. We had to get over the fear, as even if he did come by car, he had to get out of the car, perhaps at the vet's, parked beside a four-lane main road; perhaps in a large car park, on our way to somewhere else; outside friends' houses, all on roads along which cars came by fast. And what use is a dog you can't take anywhere?

One day a particularly noisy and alarming lorry with a huge cement mixer came by, rolling as it went, rumbling as it went, and Janus stood rock still. I knelt beside him; which is the advice given in the Home Office manual for police dog handlers when training a nervous dog; and what is good enough for them is good enough for me. I coaxed, and he decided that after all, he would walk on.

'Come on, feller. It won't hurt. You're safe with me.' Anything at all so long as it was the right tone, the reassuring tone. I could have murmured 'rhubarb, rhubarb' or 'buttercups, oats and mustard seed'; it wouldn't have made any difference but it would have sounded even odder, so we stuck to words that meant something.

46

As it was, I couldn't win.

A woman passed me, beside her a little boy who turned, as little boys do, and stared at me with penetrating eyes.

'Who is that lady talking to?' he asked at the top of his voice.

'Her dog.'

'Why?'

His mother turned and looked at me, giving me a look of pitying contempt, said 'God knows', and walked on.

I can't think why it is considered insane to talk to an animal. Those who really understand animals know it is not. If people who don't have dogs and who visit me would only open their mouths and say 'Good dog. It's only me,' through the door, instead of expecting the dog to know who it is by magic, the dogs would stop barking. As it is people stand like stuffed dummies, offended because the dogs haven't recognised them at once as not being burglars.

I was finding Janus hard going. It was time to seek out that dog club and take him for lessons and get help. Only I had an unwarranted suspicion that the clubs were really only for those who are competition minded and whatever else I did with this dog, competitions would be out. It was all I could do to make him behave at all anywhere but at home.

It was almost lonelier at that time having the dog than not having him. Either he was unwell and I was bound by the routine of glucose and water and pills every few hours; or we were trying to overcome terror and it was no use doing that walking with friends as I needed all my concentration. He lunged off to smell a gate or a doorway or a tree; lunged towards other dogs; lunged away from cars that made odd noises; one with an engine like a sewing machine produced instant panic; so did people who ground their gears; lorries that came too fast towards us; motor cycles; an electric wheelchair spooked him for a whole morning; the first pram he saw alarmed him beyond

47

measure; a child on a tricycle rode into him, so that he promptly hated pavements; there wasn't one single place we could go to and enjoy. I had to be watchful, all the time.

It was very wearing.

The only people I knew with dogs had easy dogs; dogs that loved walks. Dogs that did as they were told out of the house as well as in it. Dogs without problem tummies; dogs that went to the vet once a year for a booster, or if they were very unlucky, went to have a cut paw stitched. We almost lived at the vet's. I wasn't going to admit to Kenneth and Andrew that my dog was the biggest mistake of my life, but I was feeling somewhat bitter. I looked at his pedigree. The names did not mean a great deal, but he was closely bred with dogs doubled: the same dogs on his father's and his mother's sides. Had that produced a hysterical neurotic dog? I didn't know. I still don't know. But I do know now that he has an overactive thyroid gland, which makes for excessive excitability. I wish I'd known before. It would have saved me feeling I was to blame for his odd temperament, as my worst thought of all was that dogs are supposed to reflect their owners. So—was it me?

But none of our other dogs had been in the least like this one.

I thought it high time to go to the club. Maybe they wouldn't mind if I didn't progress to higher things; but I was worried about the impression he would give, because I knew my dog was a freak; they didn't. And people judge by appearances.

They didn't know my background. They would see only the outside; an uncontrollable dog and an owner that didn't know what to do about it. I wondered if I could borrow Brandy, whom I had already trained. I thought wistfully of the walks I had had with him; long walks, going anywhere, in traffic, or out of it, with him placidly by my side, afraid of nothing, walking to heel, greeting me avidly, dying to get out on those roads. If I took him to the club the first time perhaps they would understand that Janus was a freak.

But that was idiotic and not fair to Brandy. I hadn't seen him for nearly a year; we had been much too fond of one another and it wasn't fair to go back, just the odd time, and renew an association that couldn't lead anywhere. I could never take him out with Janus. I could never take *any* dog out with Janus.

It was hard to believe, watching him round the house, that he could change so fiendishly when he came out. Jekyll and Hyde wasn't in it. The trouble was that most people saw only the fiendish side of him.

I didn't go to the dog club that week after all. My courage failed me. I was so sure no one would be able to stand my dog; I was sure he would be impossible and I would be well and truly disliked, and I knew too that they would all say the same.

'It's always the handler.'

It often is the handler, but like all sayings, that one is dangerous, it's not wise to apply it in all cases. It can lead to tragedy.

I had only recently heard of a dog that had been taken to the vet's in a sack and thrown at him, with the request to put it down. As it came out of the sack, all hell broke loose. The dog was mad; completely and clinically mad. He was two years old, and attacked everybody he saw, on sight. He had been kept locked up, and because the owners had been told it was their fault that he was like that, they had been too ashamed to seek advice. One night at the dog club had convinced them they were to blame. No other dog behaved like theirs.

When the dog was put down a post mortem revealed that its brain was almost all tumour. It had had the tumour from birth; it had suffered extreme pain, all

49

because someone had applied the old saws to its owners. 'It's always the handlers that are to blame.'

It isn't, and it's never wise to generalise, or to condemn without knowing the facts. It was a miracle that the dog never had injured anyone badly. It should have been put down months before.

I remembered that and looked at Janus and found something new to worry about. But he wasn't aggressive; he was just plain terrified, nearly all the time.

After all, everyone at the dog club *had* dogs; and all those dogs had been young once.

They would understand.

All I needed was a little help, and my dog would magically turn into a sane and sensible pooch and we'd be able to go places.

It couldn't be *that* bad.

I couldn't have been more wrong.

Chapter 5

Robert Burns wrote: 'O wad some power the giftie gie us
To see oursel's as ithers see us.'
Why on earth he wanted to, is more than I can imagine,
as it's an unchancy sort of gift, and one that many writers
do have. We are so used to writing about people, to
thinking about people, to considering other viewpoints
than our own, that we tend to look at ourselves through
other eyes; and the result is usually a massive loss of
self-confidence!

Often you know, without understanding, as however much
you try to put yourself in another's place, you can't, having
no idea of their background. I have the usual number of bad
characteristics, but one I don't have is that of envy. If my
friends do well, I really am delighted; I love to hear of a piece
of good fortune happening to one of them, and know that all
lives are made up of good luck and bad luck and no one can
avoid either. Some have too much bad luck; others perhaps
more than the usual run of good luck, but nothing lasts and
we are all a long time dead.

So though I may realise someone is looking at me with
eyes that hide either envy or pure malice (if it can be pure)
I don't understand either. It must be horrible to be so
twisted that you can't enjoy other people having a bit of
good fortune.

In the same way I knew very well what the dog club was going to think when Janus and I appeared on their horizon. Here was a typical owner, probably a fool, with a spoilt dog she couldn't control at all; probably her first dog, treated like a baby, fed on chocolates and titbits, cossetted and petted. With a dog she thoroughly deserved; a dog that ruled the roost.

I had summed up pretty accurately, I discovered some years later. In fact, I doubt if I have lived my local reputation down; others accept me as I am, but to some there I'm still the woman who made such a fool of herself when she first brought Janus to the dog club.

By now he was no problem at all at home. In fact, Kenneth and Andrew, who never took him out, couldn't see why there was any need at all to train him. He behaved perfectly; slept out of the way when told to go away and be good; played with us when we wanted him and proved, in spite of that damned tummy, to have a very sunny disposition, and to love either being a clown or playing the fool.

He knew the day's routine, and fitted into it.

'He's an admirable dog,' Kenneth said, completely converted.

Andrew thought he was great. They rioted in the garden, playing ball, or playing tag.

Dorothy took him out when I was away. I once left a note saying, 'For goodness sake take care if there are milk floats about. I don't want you to break a leg.'

She put the note back on my desk with the words 'Ha ha', added to it, evidently thinking I had somehow been accusing her of incompetence.

Next day I found another note.

'Whoops. Sorry. There *was* a milk float. See what you mean by broken leg.'

It was indeed time to make up my mind to face the dog club. I wished it wasn't held in the evening. After a day's writing and house-looking-after and working things out, I was tired.

Also I had again succumbed to my idiotic conscience and got involved with Anne Woods's Federation of Books for Your Children Groups. I thought it a great idea (I still do); I inaugurated the local group and somehow, I am never clear how, I found myself its Chairman. I am not of committee stuff; I find the formalities totally ridiculous; much of the business could be conducted in ten minutes if only people would stick to the point, which they don't, me included, as I happily chase more interesting hares with the best of them.

I was lecturing as well, and I was really far more busy than was sensible, though I hadn't yet realised that. One gets on and does things, flying from job to job, getting more and more embroiled in a rat race of one's own, without even taking time to sit and really think, What the devil *am* I doing?

I hadn't got to that stage. I was just, as one of my children used to say when small, 'onning and onning'. The dog club was yet another piece of onning. Janus was now going to the vet about once every two months instead of once every three weeks and I hoped we could avoid bugs; they would knock him out as he had very little immunity.

I summoned up all my courage and walked him up to the Parish Hall, a large and not very lovely red brick building. It wasn't a pleasant walk, as a boy on a bicycle decided to harry us by cycling right up to the dog's tail, and crossing the road when we crossed. I had yet to learn that dog club night and youth club night coincided.

I knew very well what would occur when we got there, among all those dogs.

I didn't, as it happened. Not even my vivid imagination had been able to think round Janus.

I don't know to this day whether he was impelled by panic or by wild excitement, but he pulled into that hall, at the end of his lead, panting at the top of his voice and promptly snarled himself round several dogs, some of whom were doing 'sit stays' in an orderly group. I was very busy trying to sign myself in, pay my entrance fee and my training night money, and listen as I was told I would be in Reds.

I wasn't sure what Reds were, but my face was very red as I tried to disentangle Janus from the other dogs that were there for his express benefit, obviously, and would probably any minute now leap on him and rend him apart, as what he was trying to do couldn't possibly be acceptable to them.

We careered to the end of the hall, under the gallery, where there were stacking seats. I sat, got Janus between my legs, and watched the dogs on the floor.

Good dogs. Quiet dogs. Biddable dogs, apparently all walking gloriously to heel, sitting when told, which Janus wouldn't do anywhere but at home. Outside it just wasn't on; dogs didn't do that there; or he didn't. He looked amiable, and totally unco-operative, and chased his tail.

These were dogs that had been coming for some weeks; perhaps for some months. I *was* a bit envious. It must be lovely to go for a normal walk, not career round with a high-powered lunatic.

Janus watched too.

With amazement.

And then, down the hall, in the Blues class—to which lofty height we might one day progress if we were good enough—came another dog like Janus, only this was an extremely large Afghan. It moved like an immense looping caterpillar towing its owner along. I knew a fellow feeling as I watched her try to control it. It lumbered straight towards us and Janus gave it one appalled look and crawled under my chair, fast.

The chairs behind me were empty and I had been unprepared. We went back and up, stacking ourselves neatly, until we were sitting on six chairs, or at least, I was, neatly stacked, the lead inextricably tangled round them, and my thumb painfully trapped between my chair and the one beneath.

I hated my dog with a deep undying hatred. I was going out of that hall, never to come back. I would have him put down. I couldn't stand him or this. I would get rid of him and buy something else; a hamster perhaps. Or another seal point Siamese. Or a budgerigar. I ought to have been used to absurd situations after thirteen years of Kym, but I was out of practice. There seemed to be amused faces all around us.

I know now that everyone there had some sort of bad beginning, though few had experienced anything like this.

On the floor was even worse. My hand was throbbing and it was agony to hold the lead. My arm ached and Janus progressed (if you could call it that) backwards, sideways, and in circles, pulling towards other dogs, putting his paws round them, trying to play with them or eat their ears, or catch their tails. Or else he gazed soulfully into space, occasionally lunging off at an angle towards one of the dogs lying down at the side of the hall, taking as much notice of me as of a brick wall. He took more notice of that if it had been christened by other dogs.

It wasn't possible to sit near people as he was too boisterous with their dogs. It wasn't possible to talk to people as he was overcome with gay camaraderie and tried to stand in their laps; or leap up and lick their faces. He also discovered sex, there and then, without any preliminary warning. It was an extremely interesting discovery and he didn't really mind if his victim was male, female, neutered, or not even a dog. He prefaced his sorties by a particularly evil grin. If I could only catch that expression in time, I could avert embarrassment, as a number of maiden ladies came with rather genteel dogs and they weren't at all impressed by my wretch.

55

Especially as he gloried in his misbehaviour.

I was discovering new forms of nightmare all the time. Off lead Janus would play All Round the House, and go from dog to dog along the side of the hall; he would gad off on his own in the opposite direction to every other dog; ask him to stay and he turned into a speedway racer rushing to me for safety; ask him to go down and he did, lying soulfully on his back with his legs in the air bicycling gaily and apparently madly, or else sucking his paw, eyeing me to see how I reacted to this carry on. If someone giggled, I had had it for the night, as Janus is a ham actor, and plays to the gallery all the time. He would stand on his head, bottom in the air, and gaze up at me, as if that was DOWN. Try and push him and he resisted, pushing back merrily.

For some reason too, at this time, half the dogs in the district decided to put him in his place. Possibly he was now maturing and they were determined to show this newcomer he had no place in their pecking order. He was right down at the bottom of the pack.

Unfortunately he had no intention of staying at the bottom of the pack. Though at first, he didn't understand what was happening and was bewildered.

We had to pass one house where there lived a white poodle. Poodle had a lovely little habit of charging down the drive, barking, and biting Janus on the ear.

After having one of the bites treated my vet said, 'If he won't growl at the poodle, you'll have to, or this will be a regular trip.'

It was annoying to go the long way round and not pass Poodle, so on the next occasion as he ran out, I put on my best and most outrageous growl and produced a truly magnificent noise. Janus got the idea too, and Poodle vanished, never to trouble us again.

Unfortunately Poodle's next-door-neighbour was going shopping and she came out of the gate while Janus and I were enjoying our growl together and Poodle was vanishing, quite invisible to her.

She gave us a terrified look and crossed the road. She still crosses the road if she sees me, and I have never had a chance to explain. Once more, I cursed my dog.

His next enterprise was due to a Cairn, which also bit him, racing down the field with apparent good humour which turned into an attack as soon as he came within biting range. He ran off.

A week later, on the field again, there was another Cairn. Janus was ready for it this time, and with great determination he raced down the field, reached the Cairn, tucked his nose under its tummy and tossed it into the air, and came back to me, obviously grinning.

It was a different Cairn and its owner wasn't at all amused, even when I apologised and explained. I should control my dog. Well, I would, next time, but it is very hard to stop something you don't know is going to happen. After that we kept an eagle eye open for Cairns, and he was never off lead if one was about. We cured him of his phobia years later when another Cairn owner came to the club and I explained what had happened. This owner helped me and both dogs met on leads for weeks, and lay beside one another, and now we have no trouble with the breed.

Instead he had a thing about Boxers as Sam at the club went for him twice; then Janus waded in first, whether it was Sam or not, anxious to stop the other dog going for him. Sam's owner and I got together and tried to make the dogs accept one another, but there was a deep antipathy and we couldn't trust them together. Yet either with other dogs was as good as gold. But then there are people who can't stand one another, only most of them are more devious than dogs.

Sam chatting to another Boxer is the funniest creature around, as he is extremely vocal, with a wide and expressive range, from grunt to whine, and one expects any moment to see a pointing paw come out to emphasise some fact that he is trying, so hard, to put over. Sam was as difficult at first as Janus. Boxers are delightful but they aren't the easiest of breeds.

We went on going to the dog club. By now it was necessary to go by car, as we were never quite sure what the youth club would be up to on the way home; usually it was cycles. My white coat still has a tyre mark on the back; and Janus hates cycles coming up behind him, and whips round, sure they will run into him, as several did on our walks home in the dark.

Janus caught a germ which was going round the district and had three days of violent diarrhoea and vomiting. After that we couldn't get him straight. The vet wasn't very hopeful. His bills were now even larger, not because he was unreasonably expensive, but because I had a dog that seemed to need constant attention. If he didn't get it, he lost condition fast; he was never plump, at the best of times.

I was increasingly busy, writing now partly to help pay those bills; I felt very guilty about them. And the vet had to come to us, and house visits cost a lot, even in those days. I was permanently tired.

Yet there was work to do, all the time; books to write, publicity occasions, like Children's Bookshows; one in London, another involving a week in Dublin, where I met Noel Streatfeild, whose books had enthralled me and then my own daughter. I listened to her enchanting the children each afternoon, before my own turn to talk.

I was travelling all over the North West circuit, talking to luncheon groups of various sorts; travelling seemed to involve overnight stays and most of the luncheons seemed to be on a Tuesday so that Monday nights became more and more difficult. Then the Book Group decided Mondays were their best night, and Janus had very little training, and he needed it more than ever, now, when we went out.

Brian, a friend of mine, who owns two Jack Russells, Patch and Scoot, suggested I came to Wilmslow, with him and his wife and their dogs, as that was on a Wednesday and my Wednesdays were much freer. I was usually home by then.

I changed clubs and went to the Wilmslow training club in the Parish Hall in Water Lane. We hadn't really got very far, but we did progress from Reds to Blues. And there we stuck as Janus had no intention whatever of doing a 'stay' off the lead; and as for walking to heel off the lead ... I had to be joking. He could barely walk to heel on the lead anywhere except in the garden and he did it so well that I felt more and more frustrated as I watched him play the fool at Wilmslow.

One of the trainers there was Eric who has his own security business now, but then was just starting up. I was talking to him one night, telling him that Janus was only unbiddable in public and he offered to give me a few private lessons.

We went down to a local playground and worked there. Janus responded where it was quiet with no other dogs to distract him, and after six of Eric's lessons we came second in a club competition in the Blues, which cheered me up a bit, though in the lower classes it is the handler that gains the marks, and not the dog.

By now Eric knew a bit more about me and a lot more about Janus. His advice wasn't very helpful. Put him down. Or shoot him. Said with a laugh, but I suspected more than half seriously meant. Eric, who is tall and dark and burly, knows dogs and works with them, and he can't afford to keep a lunatic; I wasn't prepared to give up yet, though I was now pretty sure I was batting all the time on a losing wicket. At home, Janus was all that any dog should be.

I supposed I could leave him at home, but I was tired of going everywhere entirely alone and the dog was company. Also, he guarded my car.

Mostly, club nights are pretty busy; some people on the floor, others sitting quietly; many come with friends, and conversation is difficult, as there are commands being given by the trainers, those who are working are talking to their dogs, and it's generally pretty noisy. I enjoyed my lessons with Eric and enjoyed talking about dogs.

On one occasion, while we were still having extra lessons, Janus and I went down to the local field on Highfield Road for exercise. There was an Alsatian running free. I had never seen him on the field before; he raced up to us barking, and I wasn't sure that he didn't intend to attack. Janus was quite sure. He knew the dog was about to attack, and pulled backwards. I tripped, banged my head on a tree, fell into some stinging nettles and lost all my keys. It was summer. My head hurt and my bare arms and legs were painful.

I was far from polite to the Alsatian's owner. She assured me he meant no harm, and I know now he didn't, but it *is* unnerving when a large strange dog races up to you, barking, even if his tail is wagging; you don't look at that end. I remember the incident and try to make sure my dogs don't transgress.

I decided to avoid the field when the Alsatian was there and went down next day at seven in the morning, only to find his owner had had the same idea and we met again.

'Well, I *did* try,' she said. We grinned and parted.

We met some months later at a neighbour's wedding, without our dogs, and found we got on very well.

Meanwhile I picked myself up, but could not find the keys anywhere. Luckily Dorothy was at my home. I was able to get in, and I had spare car keys, but I don't like house keys adrift. I rang Eric, who came down with his tracking dog, Zimba. Unfortunately, in hunting for the keys myself I had fouled the ground thoroughly. My scent lay everywhere, and the dog couldn't find them. I changed the locks, and now none of my cases will lock and neither will my desk.

Next door to this piece of ground is a playground, well fenced and gated. Eric knew that Janus defied me when off the lead, and wouldn't come. So we went together to the playground, and closed the gates firmly, and let Janus run free. Eric enticed him into a corner and I slipped away and hid.

Eric stopped the game, sat down on a bench and watched the dog. Janus sniffed at the ground, and then came to look for me. But I had gone. He ran, more and more frantic, from gate to gate, searching everywhere. No sign of me.

I was safely hidden outside the gate, and after a few minutes came in again. I was greeted with frantic joy, and after that, the dog took very good care to check on me, and make sure that I was near. It's no use trying this alone, or without a safely fenced area, but where it is safe it's an excellent way to teach a reluctant dog to come when he's called or he might find himself on his own.

Some days later I drove down to Bexhill to visit my parents, taking the dog with me. My father had lost weight, tired easily and was far from well. I didn't like his symptoms at all, and worried about him when I got home. Also Janus was now thinner than ever too. So thin that I didn't know how he managed to stay alive.

So thin that someone came across to me one evening, furious, accusing me of starving the dog, of not knowing the first thing about Retrievers, of not being fit to have a dog. I was too taken aback to answer then and there; it was grossly unfair, as he didn't know me and he didn't know a thing about my dog. But people are always only too ready to jump to conclusions and to base their opinions on guesses, rather than facts.

61

It didn't help at all; nothing I could do put weight on the dog, and he remained wildly excitable. Sometimes, lying awake at night, common sense told me I ought to have him put down; but he wasn't in pain and at home he was always delightful; and we were all attached to him. I couldn't make up my mind. I couldn't accept defeat. I couldn't bear to part with him; not at just over one year old.

Yet when I looked at him I was aware of all his difficulties; his coat was harsh and whatever I did, adding cornoil to his food, brushing him vigorously, it made no odds. He was long in the leg and so thin he looked like a deformed greyhound. I not only had a dog that appeared to be a temperamental mess; he was also a physical wreck.

He went back to the vet and this time proved also to have a kidney complaint, so he had yet more pills. Perhaps that was the cause of his present slipping back.

It was January and it was cold. Christmas was a memory and spring was a long way off. I was due for a lesson but when we started I was so apathetic that Eric looked hard at me and said, 'Get in the van'.

It was a small red van, like the police dog vans; Zimba was behind the dog-guard and barked at me and Eric's young longhaired dog, Zorra, was there too. I got into the passenger seat, with Janus lying at my feet, and we sped down the Cheshire lanes, where I lost all sense of direction.

'Where are we going?' I asked.

I got Eric's funny grin, when he's about to play some kind of joke or leg pull.

'You'll see when you get there.'

I recognised the Ilford factory at Mobberley. We passed it and turned into a long lane I had never noticed before; down the lane to the end, across the road to Ashley and into another lane guarded by a notice reading:

'Private. No Through Road.'

Into that lane and then to another notice:

'Gorsefield Alsatians.'

It meant very little then; I had never heard of them; I knew little about the breed. I looked at the lovely sprawling red-brick farmhouse; the cobbled yard and the big barns and a lordly Alsatian in his pen by the gate, barking at us.

Gorsefield Salvador Marksman.

Marcus.

It was another name that was to mean much more to me later. There were Alsatians everywhere, tails waving, some barking, all delighted to see Eric who obviously knew them well.

Inside the house was a welcoming atmosphere, a big friendly room, the floor of it seemingly covered in dogs. Ziggy, an Alsatian bitch; Bleep, a long haired chihuahua, guarding everybody including the Alsatian; two sleek delicately made little whippets, and a number of cats. I am never sure which were in then, but among them was a lynxpoint Siamese, the first I had seen; a velvety Burmese named Black Secret who later disgraced herself by her own secret, producing four ginger and black kittens instead of the pedigrees she was supposed to have; and a big gorgeous tabby named Moggie.

And Judy Pilling.

Judy had read most of my books; and she breeds Alsatians. She had bred Champion Gorsefield Granit, who features in the encyclopaedias on dogs that influenced the breed. She took me into a new world, of dog shows, of champions, of breeders and of handlers. She talked dogs; dog psychology; funny dog incidents; dog lore and dog information. My head was spinning.

And she took me out to see Jasmine and her daughter Witch.

Wise Jassie, with her lovely sensitive face and watchful eyes; and little gentle Witch who won't have her pups unless her mother comes too, so all Witch's pups have a babysitter as well as their mother; Jassie helps look after

63

them. Jassie was retired. Witch was to have two more litters; she would be mated in a few months to Tarquin of Dawnway, who was then not yet a champion, but was a lovely-looking dog.

Dog shows were beyond my knowledge. I had never even been to one.

I fell in love with Witch.

Eric had told Judy about Janus. She suggested that I should bring him out and exercise him in her fields, which are well-fenced, since town walks were such a nightmare; walk him round quiet Mobberley lanes and come back for coffee. If I liked I could walk some of her young stock.

It was early in 1972, the beginning of one of the worst spells in my life, and I was floating in a limbo due to my own indecision. I ought to put Janus down and try again with a healthy dog; and I simply couldn't bring myself to do it.

I asked Judy's advice.

She is like me; her veterans live on, comfortable and cossetted, looked after till death comes naturally for one reason or another or euthanasia is imperative. She can't bring herself to put down a bitch that isn't producing; or a stud dog past his best. She feels he has earned his keep. In a way, she reassured me; I wasn't being so stupid after all. Or if I were, I wasn't the only one to be soft-hearted. Someone breeding professionally could be just the same.

She knew something was wrong with my dog, which did make up for those at Wilmslow who simply believed I starved him.

I was introduced to Judy's partner, Jess Moores, who breeds the Velindre Alsatians, down in Herefordshire. At that time Judy, Jess, and Rita Spencer shared Ch. Druidswood Consort, a beautiful sable stud dog, who died last year. When I went to my parents I could stop the night with Jess, and there I got to know her husband, Bert, who has farmed, though he is now retired (supposedly) and is full of country wisdom about dogs and all farm animals.

64

It was he who told me the old rhyme about horses.

One white sock, try it,
Two white socks, buy it.
Three white socks, look well about it.
Four white socks you're best without it.

I wasn't sure it was true as Lymm Sovereign who was then the best Shire horse in Britain had four white socks.

Visiting Judy was the brightest thing about my life that year. There were new pups and we hung over the kennel door, watching them as they tumbled and bit one another and bumbled about, staggering on roly-poly legs, totally self-absorbed, unaware of any of the trials we humans were enduring. Judy herself was overworked and over-tired at that time and needed more help than she had, though Sheila was marvellous and Marian came whenever she could. But help was needed to build kennels and do repairs and keep the place in order; it is a huge place with large barns and outhouses and twenty-eight acres of ground and Judy's husband, Les, has a full-time job of his own. Something always needed doing.

Mobberly is not near shops either; it's a fair run to Altrincham or to Knutsford. My life seemed easy compared with Judy's; writing was child's play compared with looking after all those dogs and she had horses too; though later, when we came to write a book together, Judy found that it isn't really as simple as that. I wrote and she rewrote, corrected and arranged, and ended up mentally exhausted as well.

That year, we all seemed to have plenty of spare time. Eric was just beginning his own business; he had rented a dilapidated cottage, derelict and vandalised, and was renovating it. It's beside the park where I walked Janus. Sometimes I called in to see how work progressed and sat on a dustbin, among piles of wood and floor tiles, drinking coffee, surrounded by Alsatians.

Judy's vet was about to put up his plate near me; and

had time to spare; I had Dorothy to help me and could get away more easily. We all met, perhaps once a week, in the Chapel Inn or the Bull, to eat beef butties or baked bean toasties and drink according to our likes; I usually chose lager and lime, and we drank and talked dog with Janus and pups at our feet, while Judy and Eric argued about the merits of one dog or another, not always agreeing. Eric handled Judy's show dogs, and lots of the talk was of the last show and the next one and which dogs were to be entered.

'That show? Shah? But what's the use; you know the judge doesn't like his type.'

There are several types of dog in every breed; some judges like one type and some another; Northern dogs differ from those in the South; the standards alter, almost imperceptibly, as judges influence the breeds by their choice. It's a waste of money for a breeder to show a dog under someone who doesn't like that type at all. Yet it's not in the least crooked. Some of us like milk chocolate and some prefer plain, but both are chocolate.

I listened wistfully. I wasn't going to have an Alsatian; I already had Janus. I remembered my childhood dreams, of breeding pups of my own; of having my own brood bitch. Janus was having one of his bad spells, back at the vet, no walks and no training. I was walking Witch, who was now in whelp, taking her gently round the lanes, liking her more and more each day, as she came to me confidently and confidingly, knowing we were off out, a lovely change from kennels and lying in the sun.

Janus would have to go. The vet bills were more than fifteen pounds a month. It was ridiculous to keep him. He lay in my car, without much energy. He lifted his head when I came and crept to my feet, and leaned against my knee, and wagged his tail and licked my hand.

I had almost made up my mind to ask the vet to put Janus down, when there came an invitation from Corgi to go to the Children's Book Show at Liverpool as their author representative. Richard Robins, the publicity manager at that time, could come for me, or I could meet him there.

Publicity functions can be awful ordeals, as times don't work out, and things go wrong and bookshops seem to forget that authors are human, but I always enjoyed doing them with Richard as he has a sense of humour and we could laugh together about the ghastlier bits: like getting stuck in a lift at the old BBC buildings in Piccadilly, Manchester, and the drunk who parked across our car when on the way to Liverpool, delaying us for so long that by the time the police had sorted it out we were already late and arrived after our audience had given us up for ever.

Corgi paid for a car to take me there, as Janus had to come too. Dorothy was on holiday and there was nobody to look after him and I had no idea what time I would return. At least if he were with me, I could slip out and walk him, and he could stay in Richard's car. He was safe in cars and didn't chew the upholstery.

Richard was coming home with us and staying overnight.

It was very sunny, but we found some shade, and parked and left the dog outside. Puffin was there, with Alan Garner and a load of gimmicks. We were in a different room, with very few children coming in to see us. I looked out of the window. The car was no longer in the shade and the room *was* shady. Also we were so much on our own I wondered if the organisers would mind if I brought in the dog.

Surely, bring him in.

In he came, glad to be out of the car, bounding eagerly up the stairs, sniffing at this strange place which didn't smell at all of dogs. He was used to going to dog club; always dogs there. No dogs here. Oh well.

He settled down at my feet.

A small girl looked in and vanished.

The whisper went round.

Joyce Stranger's in there. She's got a *dog*.

To this day I'm sure Puffin believe it was a deliberate gimmick. I had not realised the attraction of a live animal. A dog. A curly effusive Teddy Bear of a dog, suddenly blossoming. He offered his paw. He butted at small hands, he glowed with pleasure as hands caressed him; he put his ears back and sat there, eyes half closed, blissful, soaking up admiration.

'Isn't he lovely?'

'Isn't he *good*?'

He rolled on his back and sucked his paw. We were inundated by children trying to get at him and cuddle him. I don't remember if they bought any books. Mostly book shows are wonderful occasions to talk to the children, but very little else. I was too much absorbed in discovering that my dog was a born showman.

I knew at the end of that day that I couldn't put him down. Not because he was a commercial asset; but because he had such a lovely temperament and had behaved himself so incredibly well. It was only near traffic or among other dogs that his fiendish personality developed. Never mind the horrors he committed then; he could come with me on publicity occasions, could stay in the hotels, making the long evenings alone less daunting; I *would* take him out and about.

And there was still, even now, the faint hope that I could get him well.

Chapter 6

We continued to go to Wilmslow Dog Club whenever possible. It socialised Janus, even if he didn't show much progress. We went up to Greens, which meant he could do a stay without getting up and running off the floor, or to me; he had his moments, but mostly he did try. He showed signs of being an extremely clever dog, but only to me. Everyone else was liable to say, 'Oh, Janus. You know *him*.'

I also now knew that Janus was fighting me, away from home, all the time, because he wanted to be pack leader. I didn't realise it at first; dogs are cunning, and this one of mine had brains, though they were dog brains, not human ones, and that was where the trouble lay, as I don't think like a dog. And I had to learn how this one thought, as a dominant dog is a very different animal from a quiet submissive 'never challenge anyone' dog. He couldn't win at home, or on lead—he *could* win when he was in a large area, and free. And he was black determined.

Looking back at my working diary for that year, I realise now that my life was very complicated indeed; I was overworking, but that hadn't occurred to me. The dog ensured that we had trips to the vet; as well as his normal care and exercise. There were publicity functions, and I have a number of publishers, as I am a full-time writer, and prefer writing to many other occupations; I don't sew or knit, or embroider; and I have to keep my brain busy, because it's that kind of brain; if I am not actively writing, I am plotting a new book, or an article, or a short story; only when I am working a dog can I switch off.

I was broadcasting book reviews once a week for Radio Manchester; was very involved with the Children's Book Groups, running ours, opening new ones, going to sell children's books, or talk as an author to other groups, organising a Book Show in Cheadle Hulme; answering letters about children's books; answering the phone when people rang wanting to know what to give a dim five-year-old or a brilliant six-year-old or a nonreading eleven-year-old. Answering the phone to committee members who seemed to think I did my writing by remote control, not realising I sit down daily, come rain, shine, fair or foul weather, and set myself a target of words that *must* be written. It might not be good enough tomorrow, but at least I have tried.

Take time off, and it's far too difficult to force yourself back to the long lonely hours spent working out those stories which others will read, and some will write and say they enjoyed, making up for the time spent, and the research done, and the difficulties that inevitably come when you try to write consistent stories. Time is my bugbear, as I find I have a boy aged five and a dog aged one and by the end of the book the boy is still five and the dog has aged, or vice versa. And what flowers bloom in March? And are there nightingales in Scotland? And what colour *is* a pheasant's egg?

My kind of book can't be written off the top of one's head.

On June 21st of that year I took Janus on what proved to be the first of a series of annual visits to Reddish Vale Comprehensive School, to talk to the children in their first year about writing and about animals.

70

Janus was supposedly not quite five months old, according to his records. But·Janus was almost full-grown, and when the children clapped he pulled me off the stage through the rear curtains. We made a fresh entrance, and this time he did behave, and settled down very well. I had the kittens with me, in their travelling cage. The children here live in urban surroundings and animals are a rare treat.

We have now been five times. Betty Gillman, the librarian, has become part of my life, visiting us and cat sitting if I am away, spoiling Chia and Casey very thoroughly. She can't have animals, as she is out all day and away in the holidays, so she borrows mine. One day, she will have her own.

Kenneth at that time was in America.

He always seemed to be off somewhere: Toronto, Montreal, Washington, New York, Frankfurt, Zurich, Munich, Geneva, Paris, Moscow.

I was still travelling the North West circuit for the lecture agency: Darlington, Whitehaven, Redcar, Harrogate, Leeds, Newcastle, Preston, never such glamorous places as Kenneth! Sometimes stopping overnight; often all day in trains, just to talk for about three-quarters of an hour to people after they had eaten their lunch.

The talks took time to write and time to rehearse and the same one, in my field, doesn't do for all audiences as country people don't need the kinds of explanations you may have to give to town people. They know what tups and steers and cleansings are.

I rarely thought about what I was doing; there wasn't time.

It might have gone on till I dropped exhausted if it hadn't been for one very remarkable occasion at a place some distance away.

At that time the railways were playing silly games and you never quite knew if there would be a train or not; I had gone one morning for the Manchester Pullman, intending to go down and see how my parents were getting on.

No trains.

But if committed to a lecture you have to get there, no matter how. I did not want to drive myself; I find it far too exhausting to navigate in strange places, contend with the traffic, find a hotel in a town full of one-way streets, eat among strangers, talk for three-quarters of an hour, and then set off again on a long journey home, totally drained of energy.

Kenneth agreed that it was not sensible when I did mention it one night, as the possibility of no trains bothered me.

Then we discovered there would be trains after all, and I wrote to organise myself, saying I would arrive on the train that got in at twelve-two. I received a letter back saying that wouldn't do as they lunched at 12.30, needed to talk to me first and it left very little time. Would I please get the train from Manchester that got in at 11.15.

Which was all very well, but it happened to mean leaving home about six; and getting up at five; and it was going to be a very long and tiring day. Then Dorothy pointed out that I would be away from six a.m. till midnight, and she would be on holiday, and Kenneth was going away and what about Janus?

Take a car, Kenneth said. It's ridiculous to mess about like that. If you have a driver he can walk the dog while you're busy; and for the little amount of money you salvage from these jaunts, what does it matter if you are out of pocket for once?

I rang the taxi firm. Yes, I could have Sid for the day. Sid would be a godsend as he knows a lot about racing; and I was writing about a racehorse (Zara); Sid would be fine for Janus. It would cost five pounds more than the fee, but so what? It would be a sight more comfortable than a hot and crowded train—or worrying if the train didn't run at the last moment.

I wrote to say I would be arriving by car, and received a letter asking me to be sure we were early.

The gods that laugh at travellers were out in force that day. It was a scorcher, and I was wearing a pale green nylon silk two-piece dress and coat that was far too hot. It was a Ladies' Luncheon, which meant a hat, which was mentioned specifically in my instructions. I had my hat with me, a feather affair with a boa; as I normally live in jeans and shirts I was uncomfortable. I had old shoes for the drive and my good ones behind me on the seat, just praying I wouldn't do as a friend did and forget to put them on. My old ones definitely weren't Ladies' Luncheon shoes.

The sun blazed on us. The dog panted. I walked him in a layby, much to the lorry drivers' amazement; dressed up for a garden party, in flat old shoes, Janus doing one of his major 'I'm in a panic' acts, and nothing else at all. Sid had never driven that way before and nor had I so we didn't know there was a toll gate; or that the traffic slowed to a standstill as people hunted for change. It added nearly an hour to our journey and the minutes fled by and I got more and more edgy and we couldn't find the hotel which seemed to be the wrong side of all the one-way streets.

We arrived. Sid slid off thankfully with the dog, and vanished, leaving me marooned among unwelcoming strangers. I had remembered to change my shoes and I was clutching my hat and felt hot, sticky and very uncomfortable, as well as slightly sick.

'You're late.'

I apologised. It was almost twelve; but we had left home at seven-thirty and it's very difficult indeed to time a journey on strange territory. There wasn't a motorway then.

I washed and put on my hat.

'That's a hat and a half, isn't it?'

It wasn't a remark to put a slightly unnerved author at her ease.

I chose neat whisky, hoping it might settle my rebellious inside.

'I have had a terrible morning because of you. Collins didn't tell me they were changing the publication date of your book to bring it out today.'

I murmured that they hadn't told me, either.

'You are not here to advertise your books. You are here to entertain my ladies. I won't have the books mentioned, and I have stopped the Press from coming. I had exactly the same trouble with Alan Melville and Godfrey Winn.'

I reached blindly for my glass, hysterically unsure whether I had just been promoted or demoted. And also aware that if they had been recent speakers, I was going to fall flat on my face as I am not a practised speaker. Most people want me because they have read the books.

Also I talk about my books; it's usually what I'm there for; and what the blazes was I going to talk about if I couldn't mention the books? I meekly trailed in to lunch.

The room was lined by French windows, all behind me; the sun blazed through and there was a long mirror opposite. Lunch was Dover sole and chips and peas and some sort of steamed pudding with custard and I couldn't face any of it. The sickness was still there and now I had one of those thumping headaches that feels as if goblins are inside your skull operating steam hammers.

I thought of Sid and Janus, somewhere out in the cool of the park, with sandwiches and a tin of beer.

I asked if I could have salad and an ice cream. It didn't help, but I got it.

Then I stood up to talk. My brain went blank. All I could think of was book titles. I had prepared my talk some days before and rehearsed it, and now I was expected to change at short notice; and there I was with my head full of the people I had met for the *Breed of Giants*; and those who helped give rise to *The Running Foxes*; and the book that had been published that day. I tried and dried up. Words stuck in my throat, it got hotter than ever, and I thought of Alan Melville bewitching everybody and Godfrey Winn and wished there was a Royal Society for the Prevention of Cruelty to Authors. I wasn't an entertainer; and I was not going to go through any more of these ordeals. There was one more booked for two weeks later, and I was going to resign. My father's illness gave me a good excuse.

I managed something, and commented that it was far too hot to bore them with a long talk, and sat down. The local radio station asked if I would go round there and had been told I wouldn't; by now I was so irritated I decided I would. I hadn't been asked. The refusal had been made without consulting me at all.

I found my way and arrived.

'We didn't think you'd come. We were told you were *very* awkward.'

Words failed me. The interview, though, went splendidly and I was much happier when I found Janus and Sid, and we went home, talking of realities. I wasn't going to be used again.

Though the next luncheon nearly made me change my mind; I can't remember now where it was; somewhere in the Midlands. They were charming, meeting me, introducing me to people, taking me back for my train afterwards, concerned for my comfort.

The most interesting of all those engagements was in Keswick, where I was reported as being guest at a Literary Luncheon the next year; and even what I said. I often wonder who *was* guest, as I have never been to a luncheon anywhere in the district, not even invited to one, and that particular day I spent out at Mobberley. I stole someone's thunder!

By now I had become interested in training. I was making a little progress with Janus; I might have been quicker if I had known that he was not a run of the mill dog, and that the normal training methods just wouldn't work for him; they needed adapting. No one else had time to analyse my dog; the basics of dog training do for the majority of dogs; unfortunately they aren't usually the dogs that give trouble. Clubs really need a troubleshooter; someone who has had a great deal of experience with difficult dogs; but there just aren't many such people about. Those that do have experience of that kind usually have full-time jobs connected with dogs and very little time to spare outside them. By now I had become intrigued by the problems involved in training a police dog. This couldn't be as easy as it seems when you see the finished product. Collins/Harvill, my publishers, were interested in the idea and Sir William Collins wrote to ask the Chief Constable at Chester if he would provide me with the facilities to ensure I got the facts right.

I had an interview to make sure I didn't intend to use the material I got to attack the police for their training methods, or for some other unreasonable purpose. All I wanted was to write about the dog and a dedicated man; I wasn't interested in making up a story about bent coppers, or some sensational but grossly unfair plot.

I took a special constable's course to learn a little about police work. I had never realised how much law a policeman must know to do his job properly. He might arrest someone innocent; or arrest them for the wrong crime if he didn't know the difference between larceny and taking away without the owner's consent.

One night everyone was amused because there had been a report of an eagle flying loose in a Stockport park. Out went those who were free to hunt for it. And then someone asked, 'What do we do if we catch it?' More to the point, could they catch it? It flew off, leaving everyone rather thankful it had gone. It can't be very easy to arrest an eagle.

Soon after that I spent some days with the Cheshire police, talking to the men about their dogs; watching the dogs training in normal obedience; Janus and I joined in briefly when the lesson had ended, just to see how he shaped. Not very impressively!

I found it fascinating to talk to the men; to watch the handlers train and work; to go over to the Training Centre and talk to them and meet their dogs and listen as they discussed real life tracks, some of them pretty gruelling for man and dog. This isn't trials or competition; this is work, man and dog continuing in all weathers, all night if necessary, never giving up while the scent is hot.

There were lessons to be learned about training my own dog. No police dog is ever allowed to fail, even when he is fully trained. He is also given frequent refresher courses, because dog memories are short and they soon forget.

If the dog goes into a building to find a crook, and the man has gone, a policeman or some other volunteer hides, so that the dog's search ends in success; otherwise he will become discouraged and not try next time. What's the use of hunting for somebody who isn't there?

It taught me to make sure that when I teach my dogs, if I am trying something new and difficult, and the dog gets bewildered, probably because I haven't yet found out how to get over to him just what I want, then we go right back to something he can do and that gives him immense pleasure. With Janus, it's carrying something of mine, be it newspaper or letters or my glove. He's been puzzled and unhappy and we change the tune; up go his ears and he comes proudly, doing something he fully understands, tail wagging, eyes glowing, totally confident.

Next time I want him he'll come eagerly. What are we doing now? More fun? OK, I'm game.

The police are one of the most helpful organisations for

any writer; they like you to get things right. All the time I was writing that book, one or other of the handlers called in to make sure I had no problems and to help me plot tracks and handle incidents correctly. One of my neighbours, I suspect, thought I was under surveillance and knocked to ask if we had had a burglary or something. No, I was writing a book about a police dog.

Curiosity satisfied, he went away!

Janus was a major help in writing that book. I was able to use some of his training problems for my police dog, describing my hero's problems with his fictitious dog, knowing that it isn't just a matter of saying 'sit' and the dog sits; of showing him once and he knows. Most dogs have to be shown again and again and again. Some never understand at all. Some handlers and some dogs never make a team, yet change the handler and the dog settles down.

One of the places where I watched the police search was a disused prison camp near Warrington; broken down Nissen huts; bleak waste ground, rough, dry strawlike grass and a moaning wind. It was the end of the world; total desolation; the scene of a thousand possible crimes in a thousand different books.

One of the sergeants asked me how the book ended. I had planned a simple track with one dog.

'Couldn't you do an all-out search involving all the dogs and men? It's one of the most interesting things to do, especially if we're successful. And it's the one time we can meet and compare notes and dogs.'

It sounded difficult but they promised to help me, so I learned how to mastermind a major search; how they set it up, and involved all the dogs and men in the area. Talk of dogs was wonderful; I had much of it at first hand; talk of the vagaries of scent, one of the most baffling things to a man. How can a dog detect a quarter ounce of cannabis in a midden? How the dog tracks; the feel of the search and

78

the cold and the rain and bad ground and the lonely roads at night.

The lonely roads at night.

I took to walking Janus at midnight round the quiet houses; night sounds, and the wind in the trees, an owl hooting, an odd patch of light, a disconsolate child crying, and only cats abroad. The terror inspired by a cat yowling suddenly in the bushes and the lurking shadows that bend and sway as trees dip in the wind.

The dog at my side, surprisingly steady. There is very little traffic at night. He baulked at first at shadows between the lampposts, shadows that grew and died away and sprang suddenly up at him along a wall. He kept close against me, perhaps as edgy as I, wondering at the footsteps behind me, at the bulk against a wall that proved to be a dustbin, put out for the men in the morning.

There were sometimes lights; a mother with a sick child? An old woman or an old man lying near to death? Someone unable to sleep?

Down the lonely roads, and I remembered the poem:

> As one who on a lonely road
> Doth walk in fear and dread
> As if he thought some fearful fiend
> Did close behind him tread.

Walk A Lonely Road. What else could I call the book? Thinking back, those policemen who watch over us earn every penny they get; it's no kind of joke, out there in the dark while everyone sleeps, waiting for the unlawful to startle the night into violence.

The book was finished at last. Life was still complicated by Janus's visits to the vet, by that impossible inside of his, that seemed to suffer from one virus after another, the last hardly gone before another started. Or was it something else?

The vet began to wonder and so did I.

It would have been easy if he hadn't been such a gentle

dog at home. He was still wild away from home, but most of our life was lived between four walls or in the garden; most of his day was spent with me, just the two of us. The cats are self-sufficient, not needing us except when it's cold and they seek a lap.

He was gay when he was well; and he was absurd. One winter day we judged a children's fancy dress parade, which Ted Horwood, of 'This and That' in Cheadle Hulme precinct, had arranged. Ted himself was the front half of a pantomime horse.

Janus knew horses. Judy had them in the field and he ran among them, ignoring them, occasionally stopping to look up at one, or sniff one. The horses were used to dogs. He watched the pantomime 'horse' cavort, was a little surprised when it trotted up to us and rubbed its head against my cheek, making the children laugh.

We judged the dresses, which was difficult as parents had gone to immense trouble to make them, and the standard was very high. It's an impossible task and someone is sure to be unhappy, but at last I made up my mind. The children took their prizes and went away.

'Cor, it's hot in here,' Ted said, and removed his head and put it at Janus's feet.

I have never seen a dog so astounded. He stared at the head, stared at the man and watched as the skin was sloughed and two men stepped out of it. He sniffed at the horse 'skin' lying on the ground.

Two days a later a horse trotted past us on the road. Janus sat and watched, eager, expectant, his eyes delighted, waiting hopefully, I am sure, for it to stop and remove its head. It was months before he ceased to watch every horse we met, lest it had the same peculiar habit as Ted.

Some weeks later, visiting a friend of mine whom he had not met before, he did the same thing with a cuckoo clock.

He obviously thought Cuckoo splendid, and watched it avidly, inching closer and closer until he was sitting right underneath it as it leaped out, counting eleven.

He sat, waiting, eyes unmoving, watching the doors for the next quarter of an hour, and was rewarded this time by one call for the quarter. He remained on guard, waiting, all through our visit and next time took up his stance again, wanting to see the little bird that flew out and called to him.

He was capable of immense patience.

One day I lost him. I hunted the house, calling, but no dog came. I found him at last in the kitchen, looking down at four dog biscuits that had somehow, mysteriously, got on to the floor, probably through the machinations of one of the cats.

There were tears in his eyes and a pool of saliva on the floor. He had been sitting there for almost an hour and had not touched one single biscuit. He had waited until I said he could eat. I gave him the biscuits. He stood on his hind legs, putting his front paws into my hands, and touched my face with his forehead, his way of thanking me, which he still uses after he has been fed, or when he is feeling anxious, and in need of reassurance. Then, very quickly, lest I changed my mind, he wolfed all four biscuits down, and trotted after me.

So I remained unable to make up my mind to turn down my thumb and say: 'I can't afford this dog. It's ridiculous. Put him down.'

I watched him lie in the sun on his back, legs in the air; rolling on the carpet, bicycling absurdly, scratching himself on his bone; drinking, very furtively and guiltily, from the cats' tiny bowl; playing the clown at the club, shaming me, because other dogs obeyed.

The news from my father was worse, and I went down by train, unable to face the long drive while I was so worried. He was in hospital. I stayed with my mother and

Janus slept by my bed, sometimes during the day taking our minds off our worries, because he chose to turn entertainer and try to make us laugh, bringing the little toy seal that my niece had given my mother, or the koala bear that another niece had given her for a joke, or her stockings, or some other item that he dumped in her lap with an air of, 'There you are; now cheer up, do. I'm here.' His tail wagged hopefully, as he went from one to the other of us.

One thing, Janus's tummy, was almost straight, not perfect, but not giving too much trouble. He was very gassy and always had charcoal added to his food, but he seemed to be having a good patch and that was a great relief.

The second night there, I woke at two in the morning as Janus screamed.

It was a horrible noise, a cry of extreme pain. I thought his wretched tummy was playing up again and went to him. He was lying on his side, eyes wide, staring at me, lifting his head, as if trying to tell me something. I coaxed him to stand up, thinking he had better come into the garden, fast.

He couldn't stand.

He had no power at all in his hindquarters. He could fight himself onto his front legs, almost up on them, but his back legs lay on the floor, and he couldn't even turn himself over.

I didn't see what a vet could do at that time in the night; or do at all. I stretched the dog out more comfortably and put his blanket over him. I kept the light on and every time I looked down at him, those huge eyes were fixed on me, as if sure I could make him better. I stroked his head.

Morning did come, after a very long night. My mother's vet was away, but we found one, quite near, in the yellow pages, and rang him. He would see the dog at once. We carried him out to my sister's car, and had to carry him again, down a side road as we couldn't park on the main road, up one of the longest drives I have seen at a vet's and up several steps. His front legs worked, but not his hindquarters.

The vet examined him, gave him an injection, and some tablets; and then he wondered about the tablets when I produced the pills that Janus still had three times a day.

'Better not,' he decided.

'Will he be all right?'

'I should think so, in a day or two.' He was watching the dog, and so was I. Poor Janus had suffered enough. What was he in for now? And was it all part of the same thing? I didn't know and doubted if the vet knew the answer.

'What is it?' I asked.

'I should get him X-rayed when you get home. He may just have pulled a muscle; it may be something else,' he said.

By the end of the week Janus was just about fit to travel. We limped home, and once more we were off to the vet for treatment, this time for lameness. I didn't have him X-rayed then. I didn't ask questions. I didn't want to know. I would go on from day to day.

Tummy germs that lasted twelve hours for most dogs lasted thirty-six for Janus, were violent and didn't clear up without more treatment.

Training progressed backwards; there wasn't much point in training as all the time I had a sneaking feeling that one day I would just have to say: 'Right. This is it.' But not while my father was ill; there was enough to face. The dog was company and so long as I did have him treated, he wasn't suffering unduly; no more than a child with its various juvenile complaints.

He was no longer totally unmanageable. He was only partly unmanageable. He was still wildly excitable. And I mean *wildly*. If he went anywhere new he panted like a steam engine, and pulled wildly to bolt.

Yet at home he was extremely good. He adored playing with the kittens, and one day, watching me pull a string for them to chase, he took it from me, and pulled it himself, his head round to watch with a benign 'Isn't Uncle kind' expression on his face that was hilarious. He paced proudly and slowly, ensuring that they would catch the end.

On one occasion I heard the bedroom door crashing against the bedhead. Puzzled I went upstairs to find that Janus had mislaid his string and was trying to pull the girdle out of my husband's dressing gown. I gave it to him, curious to see what he would do.

At once he grabbed it, and raced downstairs, passing close by the cats. They chased the tassel and the string game began again. They could go on tirelessly and I was sorry when they all grew too sedate to indulge in such romps.

Meanwhile, my father's illness progressed slowly and inevitably and I went home as much as I could. Sometimes we drove down, the dog lying quiet, his eyes watching me, never moving. Sometimes we went by train. It was only two hours to London, where I could have coffee with my agent and go on down to Bexhill, only another two hours away. By car, it took almost the whole day.

Out at Mobberley, Witch, whom I had been walking gently throughout her whelp period, had nine most gorgeous pups. I saw them at three weeks old. Until then, Judy keeps her whelping bitches quiet, and allows no visitors in case of infection.

It was June and by the time the pups were four weeks old, they were staggering out of the whelping kennel into the run, tumbling over one another, to lie in a black and gold heap, fast asleep, or coming to the wire, begging for attention. Little bold active pups, soon running, and playing together in mock fights that sometimes turned to real, if a pup bit too hard.

Judy and I stood by the run for most of my visits,

84

watching them. One of them was gorgeous, and I fell for her completely. Merry, bold, forthcoming, a small imp, always there when I went to see them, always coming first to the wire to greet me.

It was total relaxation, away from suburbia, the sun shining, the Mobberley lanes green and beautiful. Great tits were nesting, the air was filled with birdsong and the sun shone, almost non-stop.

The pups thrived.

Janus was limping and I was walking some of Judy's other dogs; among them Klaus, one of the most sensitive Alsatians I have ever known. He couldn't even bear a raised voice. He walked placidly at heel, though he had never been trained. Janus by now had caused me to need physiotherapy for my arm which he almost pulled out of its socket. Walking him was still far from pleasure; a chore that had to be done, and endured by both of us.

The walks were all panic sessions. Help, a *tanker* and he crouched in the hedge, shivering; help, what's that? And a panicky dog tried to bolt from the first tractor he had ever seen. Cars speeding down the lanes sent him against the hedge.

My dog seemed to be the biggest coward out. I let him run free in Judy's field, getting exercise there, and went on walking Alsatians.

It was as well I had them. Janus was not paralysed again, but he went lame for the silliest reasons; once he leaped up to greet Brian at the club, and was lame for a week. Once he slipped on the club floor, and was lame again. He had intermittent periods of extreme stiffness in his hindquarters, so that I had to lift him into the back of my car; he couldn't jump. And he wasn't yet two.

The vet had diagnosed hip dysplasia.

This is a very emotive word in dog breeding circles, as it's one of those horrible hereditary things (only some say it's not hereditary) that crops up, sometimes even in

85

kennels where every precaution under the sun is taken and the breeder knows all there is to know about breeding.

Then, it's sheer bad luck and the breeder has tried, but been defeated by mating a carrier bitch to a carrier dog; and by the look of the pedigrees I have seen you can have hidden carriers, but they often are related to a dog that suffered from the complaint. Only you don't know unless you are part of the grapevine that does note these things—it tends to be exclusive. Pet owners don't belong.

I wrote an article about it in *Dog World* in August; and was intrigued this year to get a request from Mars Ltd to put a quotation from it in the Proceedings of the Australian Veterinary Society, which has now appeared. I've been promoted. I'm quoted as Dr Stranger.

'A dog is unlike any other creature. It comes into our homes and lives with us, and if it suffers, then we suffer too.'

I knew all about that. There is nothing worse than watching an animal, unable to understand, endure pain. Janus did endure; he is an excellent patient and allows any kind of treatment without a murmur, even taking pills without fuss.

I received so many letters after my article that I found myself with a number of photostat pedigrees of sound and of unsound dogs.

Breeding is a chancy business. There are people who mate dog to bitch without bothering about the ancestry of either. This may result in a good litter; it may result in a litter full of puppies with bad hips, or epilepsy, or hereditary blindness, as there are past champions that carried these in their genes and passed them on to sons and daughters. Sometimes the fault lies hidden, perhaps for generations.

But I did find one interesting fact in those pedigrees. Janus has a number of ancestors that always occur in any pedigree of a dog or a bitch of his breed with bad hips. One of them is also there if a pup goes blind. In every case of unsound dogs that I have seen, the same ancestors crop up on both sides of the pedigree, in the sire's line, and in the dam's line. Sometimes they are so far back they are off the page, but if you know enough about the breeding of the dogs, you can get back to the source of the trouble.

Yet there are a few pedigrees of sound dogs, one of them with a letter from the Kennel Club to prove he has perfect hips, in which the same ancestors appear. In every case the breeder has made sure they are only on one side; and nowhere on the other side.

The fault hasn't come out, because it needs to be on both sides before it is inherited. It may come back because a pup is bought and bred by someone else ignorant of the fault, re-introducing the faulty ancestors on both sides again. You can double without trouble if you are positive there aren't any inherited faults on either side, but according to a number of other breeders I have met, if you know there are inherited faults, then it is better to go right outside those ancestors and bring in a sound dog from elsewhere.

Faults there are, and sometimes they proliferate because someone is reluctant to admit their lovely-looking dog can produce defective puppies and does their best to keep it very dark. But it is unfair to all breeders, as then a fault can be produced in total innocence. You can't avoid something you don't know is there. If only breeders would stop hiding kennel faults, and admit them, and work to get rid of them, as the Irish Setter breeders and the working Sheepdog breeders have worked to eradicate blindness, then many of our present faults in dogs would disappear. There is no shame—unless it's covered up or denied. It's very bad luck.

Most breeders do admit there are kennel faults, are very upset when they occur, and may refund money, or offer another pup. Some breeders deny all faults, and accuse the owner, especially of a dog with bad hips. The dog was kicked, or run over, or fell downstairs. Anything but the truth.

No one is going to blame a breeder who says: 'Look, I'm terribly sorry. I don't know *how* it happens, but I do know it does happen and I'm trying to stop it.'

Most people, I would imagine, like myself, will be bitter about breeders who do not want to know, who go on breeding from stock they know is producing pups that go blind, or that go lame, or have other major defects.

Breeding is *not* a haphazard affair in the best kennels, which are not always the biggest. The breeders know which stud dogs (some of them champions) carry the worst faults, and they avoid them. Others may take a chance, because they are not concerned with working dogs, that need to be hardy and sound, but are looking for show champions.

The title champion merely means that in the eyes of three different judges the dog is the most perfectly formed there; it doesn't refer to anything inside him. He could be a devil in temperament; he could produce stock that no one would want to own. It is necessary to know a great deal about him before using him on a bitch.

Also breeding is chancy, even when you take all the care in the world, as nothing in livestock is certain. Human parents can produce mongols or brain-damaged or crippled children; dogs are bred in litters of five or more and so there is more chance of something going wrong. Yet faulty dogs are far less common than fit dogs, unless someone is puppy farming, and then the stock is often atrocious.

My own feelings about breeding were confirmed by two people. One of them sorted out the deaths of a number of Manx kittens, all so inbred that they failed to survive. The only way to stop the breed becoming extinct is to outcross.

A farmer I know, in the swine standstill order when we had an outbreak of swine fever in Cheshire, mated his sow to her own father and to quote him, he got 'fifteen monsters'. They all had to be put down. He never did it again and, using a boar on a distant farm once the order had been rescinded, the piglets were perfect.

Only yesterday I met the son of a man who has a herd of Welsh ponies. They change the stallion regularly to prevent father from mating with his daughters, so the 'blood doesn't go bad'.

Some breeders thought I was hysterical; some felt I was trying to do the breed down, but that was the last thing I had in mind. I know so many people who take enormous care to research any fault they get, and eliminate it, that it seems a crime that often, through ignorance of good breeding methods, a fault should be bred in instead of bred out, spoiling one of the most beautiful breeds of all dogs.

In all these cases, what we mean by dysplasia is different from what many breeders interpret as dysplasia; not something mild, a slight bone abnormality, but a major abnormality, and when it came to X-rays, several of them are carbon copies of Janus's hips.

I was told that we were a minority; statistically insignificant, which is as may be, but the letters I got showed me that to those of us with dogs that suffer, we are not a minority; we are a hundred per cent majority. Nor are we besotted pet owners, fussing over something that doesn't matter, as one of these who had a dog like Janus is a breeder herself, and was as upset as I that the stud dog she had bought was unusable.

He was younger than Janus, but developed severe arthritis in the hip, became vicious and had to be put down, as pain made him lash out at any animal coming near him. Breeders assumed I was condemning them without knowledge. I was not. But I would ask them to think hard before breeding too close; close breeding works if you know the stock is genetically sound. Today many are over-breeding for commercial reasons. Some of these people know very little about bloodlines so that there are animals about that should never be used for any breeding programme.

The bitch having a litter 'for her own good' may well be one culprit, as the one-off breeder doesn't know about heredity or what can happen; and may well mate her to a dog down the road that is totally unsuitable for the purpose.

One breeder I know had a supreme dog, a champion many times over, who was very much wanted at stud. She became worried by the number of bitches coming to him and by the fact that his offspring were often too closely mated, and finally sold him to someone abroad, to make quite sure that her lovely dog didn't earn a bad name through over-use or misuse.

That dog was her companion and she was very attached to him. It was a hard decision to make, but if he'd stayed here, his progeny would be so numerous that there would be a great deal of inbreeding going on. It's better to bring in strong new blood than to weaken the stock.

Another friend of mine will never breed at all from any animals that are in any way related. He goes for type; looks for a stud dog resembling his bitch, but in no way related to her, and breeds from them. The pups are gorgeous and often prize-winners at the shows.

I had letters from sad people; people whose dogs had to be put down at less than a year old; or who struggled on, and sometimes had the hip operation done. This may cure the pain; it's painful for the dog and not always successful and it is vastly expensive.

All I was ever saying was please think of the buyers of the pups. There are waiting lists for sound pups. I am on two lists; one for a German Shepherd and the other for a Golden Retriever. Not yet, but some time soon, as now I have had a chance to look round the shows and weigh up what I want, to watch working dogs and show dogs, and to know who is breeding to improve the breed, and who is only trying for profit.

Pet owners aren't all fools; our dog, to us, is as important as the champion that came from the litter bred for a good show dog; he may be the rubbish sold off, but it's not that way to those who buy him. He is still all dog and very often the dog that is imperfect physically, needing extra time and attention, develops twice as much character to make up for it. And that makes it even harder to go to the vet with a thumb turned down.

One breeder suggested I put Janus down after seeing him walk. The comment made was, 'He's a bad advertisement for the breed.' I have seldom been so near hitting anyone.

Even the vet was becoming dubious now. Janus was an expense; and a lot of work; but he wasn't in severe pain and *he* didn't know he wasn't a normal healthy dog. The family were all sold on him.

I could buy another dog. But I didn't want another dog. All I really wanted was a fit Janus. He wasn't yet two. What kind of life is that?

The periodic bouts of lameness always had cleared up. We worked out a routine. First of all rest. Then gradual exercise. Five minutes obedience heelwork three times a day; then ten minutes; then three fifteen-minute walks, gradually building him up again to take on longer walks. He can never go on a really long hike; his leg won't stand it, but we soon learned how to get the most out of his life.

No jumping.

No free running for long periods.

No lying on wet ground, or soaking in the rain when he couldn't be dried off at once, as once arthritis set in ...

I looked at Judy's healthy, lively pups, and how I longed for one. I had always wanted an Alsatian, but I had known that with them you must be careful how you pick, as some are bred to guard and they are a headache in a normal home. Most are bred for temperament but it's very important indeed to be sure about that.

Nothing could be gentler than Witch and Jasmine. Either Witchie lay with her pups, or Jassie, benignly mothering them. I came back, day after day, to stand by that wire and yearn for my own brood bitch. She came to me, nuzzling my hand, gentle and confiding, and totally enchanting. Black and gold, with enormous dark eyes.

The pups began to be sold. I had named the litter for Judy; all 'P' names; among them were Paprika and Poirot and Panther, and 'my' little bitch, Puma.

Puma.

Judy didn't want to sell her. She wanted to bring up two more dogs for stud, and Panther and Poirot, by now nicknamed Porky, were to stay. She wanted Puma too but she had several brood bitches.

'I'll have to sell her,' Judy said, one afternoon, as I watched Puma play with her brothers. She was now weaned and Witch and Jassie had returned to the adult kennel. The three remaining pups were standing against the wire, squeaking to us. 'Someone is probably coming across at the weekend,' she added.

That night at the club, Eric said he thought Judy had a buyer for Puma.

I couldn't concentrate. I could only think of Puma; of the way she greeted me; of her merry little face and madcap tricks with bones and bouncy things and with sticks, trying to carry things that were far too big for her. Bossing her brothers.

I left the club early.

I rang Judy as soon as I got in.

'Could I buy Puma and you keep her at my expense? You know what's going to happen to Janus; his tummy is worse than ever, and he's lame again.'

Judy knew only too well how I felt about that as I often landed on her saying: 'Janus can't walk this week. Can I take some of the dogs out?' And off I went with two or three Alsatians, all of them far easier on my arms than my poor goldie.

Yes, I could buy Puma. Judy would run her on for me and I could pay for her food. Perhaps I'd let Judy show her if Janus lasted another six months, and Puma looked good enough. I could come out daily and walk her, and when Janus finally went, Puma could come home; no gap and I'd know what I was getting. Her father was Champion Tarquin of Dawnway, though he wasn't a champion then; big, goodnatured and addicted to playing football. I knew Witch and Jassie well; no problems there.

I could come out and walk Puma and Panther and Porky, which would help Judy. She rarely has less than twenty dogs and it's not easy to give all of them roadwork. Another pair of hands was a big help.

I had my Alsatian brood bitch.

And I didn't have her. I wanted to take her home, but it was no use having a pup when I was commuting between Cheadle Hulme and Bexhill; she needed house training and four meals a day and more attention than I could give her.

Chapter 7

By now I was going south as often as possible. My father, though exceedingly ill, was always delighted to see me; he talked of things that went on around him; of his early years as a boy in Russia; of the war years and the battles on the Somme and the dugouts and the rain and the cold; the horse he rode; of things that happened when we were children; of the bomb that destroyed our home in 1942; of politics and political leaders and the inside reasons that he considered responsible for certain actions.

He had always been a brilliant man. He rode well; was a first-class rifle shot; spoke eight languages; had been college middle-weight champion; taught Judo; was an excellent swimmer; he wrote books; he taught unarmed combat; he filled every minute of his life and he didn't like his enforced idleness; but he never, ever complained, either at his bad luck or at the pain he endured.

Between whiles, I walked my new puppy.

I took Puma and Janus out in my car into summer lanes, where I picnicked on my own and watched him play with the pup. She was a merry little thing and it was hard to have to take her back to the kennels and leave her with her two litter brothers. It was a lovely home; she raced in the fields with the other dogs, raced against foals and calves, played amongst cattle, had the river to splash in and was walked in country lanes. But she was nobody's dog, as I was just one of a number of people who took her out or fussed her, or very occasionally fed her. There were far more important people in her life; Judy who bred her; and Sheila who looked after her; and Marian who came out at times to help; and all Judy's family. I was an extra thrown in for good measure.

I couldn't make up my mind about Janus. I decided to wait a little longer. He weighed forty-two pounds and should have weighed sixty.

Time went by.

Judy was haunted by ill luck too. She was hit by a barn door blowing shut in her face and had slight concussion which left her dizzy. Then one morning she fell and broke her leg in two places and was plastered from thigh to ankle.

I went to the dog club, but it was often a waste of time as either Janus wasn't well enough to work or I just didn't care whether he worked or not; it was good to sit and talk to people I barely knew who knew little about me. One or two knew my father was ill, and Diana, who had been through a similar experience herself, was far more help than she ever knew, coming and talking a little about her own experiences, knowing just what to say without either depressing me unduly or infuriating me by pretending everything was lovely and would be all right in the end.

Janus had another attack of violent colic. And went lame again.

My anger at breeders who *knew* of a defect and still went on was growing and that helped to counteract some of the other miseries.

I had almost decided to have Janus put down when Dorothy Steve rang me. She owned Radar, the dog that acted the police dog in *Softly, Softly*.

Her news upset me even more. I had recently finished a script for Radar; it hadn't yet been accepted, but she and I

95

both hoped that the TV people might use it. I had told her about Puma, as it was Radar who got me finally hooked on Alsatians; he was a big, magnificent, gentle dog.

'Joyce,' she said. 'Radar's dead. He died today.'

I couldn't think of a thing that was consoling to say.

'You're lucky,' I said in the end. 'You had him twelve years. I'm not going to keep Janus for two.'

I hadn't meant it as a distraction, but it worked; she began to question me about Janus, and what was wrong with him. I was feeling bitter by now, I told her.

She probably felt that I was unsympathetic.

She listened to my story. It was Janus's inside this time.

'It sounds very like Radar's trouble,' she said. 'His pancreas never worked properly. He had to have medicine all his life. I've got six months' supply left. Would you like it?'

Anything was worth a try, as by now Janus and I were extremely important to one another. Also ill luck had struck at Judy's yet again only the week before. I took Puma out; she was listless, apathetic, didn't want to come, and had an attack of diarrhoea. Not her too.

I told Judy who by now was home from hospital. Puma was segregated, but Panther and Poirot, her litter brothers, who Judy had kept, became ill as well. Poirot, usually called Porky, was a ridiculous pup; he was chatty. I walked the three of them often; Puma and Pan at heel, Porky busy exclaiming non stop in little squeals; they were growing fast and Porky was the pick of the litter. They were lovely pups.

Look, ducks!

Porky was beside himself with astonishment, pawing and squeaking to make sure I had seen too.

Look, birds!

Our walks were hilarious, total relaxation. Janus was lame again and had to stay in the car, luckily, in view of Puma's tummy trouble.

Judy's vet came; he had recently put up his plate half a mile away from me. My own vets were nearly three miles away, down Kingsway in appalling traffic; sometimes it took me almost twenty minutes to get out at the end of the road and then second gear all the way and surgery hours unluckily were in the morning and the evening rush hour. I didn't want to change; they were trying hard to cure Janus and suspected the truth; but five minutes' drive instead of forty would make so much difference and I wouldn't need house visits; I could easily be to and from the vet in twenty-five minutes at most, including waiting and treatment. House visits were now exceedingly expensive. And I was busy—it's not easy to find time to write and run a house and family. And we needed the vet so often.

Meanwhile the pups were better, but listless; little appetite, and no desire to run or walk or play; they lay, lethargic. I tried to walk Puma but she just didn't want to come. Some days she tried to get into my car; I thought for a ride and a walk, but it wasn't that. The car was dark.

The vet had no idea what was wrong.

I took Janus to him; and Radar's pills.

'No harm in trying them,' he said. 'It's one of the things I have considered, but don't hope too much. If he has what I think is wrong, it's far from simple; some dogs respond, and others don't. And he's been like it a long time.' My other vets had been saying the same thing.

'What about Puma?' I asked.

He shrugged. The pups weren't ill. They just weren't right.

Then two days later Judy rang me.

Porky was hysterical; running in circles; squealing non stop. Could I possibly get some tranquillisers and bring them out quick.

I got straight into my car and drove down to the surgery.

David, the vet, opened the door as I arrived.

'Judy's just rung,' he said. 'Porky dropped dead.' I couldn't believe it. The day before he had been full of life.

'What of?'

'I've no idea. I'm going to take his body to Liverpool for a post mortem.'

Once more we could only wait.

Janus started his new treatment; daily doses of trypsin on his food. Puma and Panther were listless, and sometimes they too were so highly excited that I dared not visit them, in case it was something Janus might catch.

The result of the post mortem was ages coming through.

Then the pups perked up and once more I began to visit.

Janus looked a little better; someone at the club commented that he was putting on weight; at last he began to digest his food properly.

I went out one morning to Judy's, to get lunch for both of us. I had brought cold chicken and salad. I put it on the plates and took it into the big friendly sitting-room, where there were dogs and cats on all the chairs.

We had just begun to eat when Panther screamed.

We had heard the day before what Porky had died of.

Lead poisoning. He had five times a lethal dose inside him. The vet was going to get an antidote and treat Puma and Pan next day, just in case. No one had the least idea where the lead had come from. Judy's own doctor was concerned and had advised the Water Board who were busy examining all the pipes.

'That's how Porky died,' Judy said, as the squealing continued.

Pan was in his kennel. I rang David. He would go for the antidote at once, meanwhile lock up the kennels; don't go near any of the dogs, and certainly not the pups.

Excitement triggered death.

We ate, after a fashion, listening. Squeals, on and on and on. And then silence. Was he dead? If I went in, Puma might start too; the other dogs howled in sympathy. Janus, in my car, cried continuously, unnerved by the weird noise and stopped and cried again.

We listened. Judy's mother, who lives in a flat attached to the farmhouse, came in to worry with us; she was even more worried because the other dogs ought to be fed and mustn't be. No one was to go anywhere near that kennel block for any reason whatever. The instructions were positive and very clear.

I made coffee. The dogs would need an anaesthetic as the antidote is thick and very unpleasant to inject and someone would need to hold them. Judy was chairbound; Mrs Mandley would have held anything but she is quite an old lady, and it was impossible for her even to consider helping. I stayed on, but rang Eric to see if he could come out.

He could, at four-thirty.

He arrived dead on time and I fled home, very late, with shopping to do and supper to get, and with no knowledge at all of what was going on.

Judy rang later that evening. Both Puma and Pan had had the antidote; Pan had been almost berserk by the time David came and it took all Eric's strength to hold him; it was a very good job he was able to come. They were both still out from the anaesthetic; Pan in the house, as he had been very bad indeed. Puma hadn't seemed so bad. They were going to have blood tests.

Next morning Pan was quite normal and Puma was eating.

No one had the slightest idea where the lead had come from. The pipes were lead, but that could not account for the high dosage Porky and Pan and Puma all had suffered; their tests showed that.

They had to be kept in the dark; had to be kept quiet; and Eric and the vet and Sheila and I walked round those kennels looking at everything we could think of for a source of lead.

99

No one thought of the obvious one until that evening, telling Andrew, he said, 'What about paint?'

We got scrapings and Andrew took them to work for a friend to test.

Lead paint. Paint, good and strong and in wonderful condition, put on years ago. Paint containing sugar of lead, to which children and pups get addicted and so do calves. Paint in a 300-year-old barn, on the wooden partitions between the dog runs.

Now I knew why Puma had to get into my dark car; had to put her head between my legs, in the dark, or run under the water trough or into a dark corner. Lead affects their eyes.

More blood tests and more antidote.

No walks; no visiting; no Alsatian pup to come with me through the lanes, and Janus still very lame, but now definitely putting on weight. Now it was important to try and adjust his diet. I knew he couldn't eat certain things, in spite of the added trypsin, which is an enzyme, made by the pancreas, which digests meat. A dog that can't digest meat is in dire trouble. Few owners would ever think of removing meat from the diet.

The pancreas also makes insulin, so this is a disability similar to diabetes. And sometimes the dog makes excess thyroid substance too—and is wildly excitable. Another clue.

It looked ironically as if Janus would survive. And Puma might not, as no one could tell us the result of prolonged exposure to lead poisoning. Fortunately none of the paint was in the whelping kennels and the whole of the litter had been sold before Puma and Pan and Porky were moved to adult quarters, so there was no need to worry about the other six pups. Puma and her brothers had stayed in the whelping kennel for far longer than normal as there were no new pups while Judy was out of action, so they had only been in the barn for six weeks; six weeks' exposure was enough to kill Porky. Luckily also the paint wasn't anywhere but in those three runs. Old sins cast long shadows, but who on earth today even dreams of lead in paint?

It is still used. Old batches in attics, or hoarded by dealers. Now we are all very careful when we buy. I wrote about this in *Never Count Apples*—partly as a warning—one never knows.

The news from Judy wasn't good and it wasn't bad. The pups were very lethargic, but they were alive. They ate; their insides seemed normal, but they just didn't respond much or play.

And then the phone went one night. My father was asking for me. Could I come, and quickly.

Kenneth put Janus and me on the first train south. There was no one at home to look after him, as Dorothy had retired. Knowing how windy the dog was we travelled first. A dog has a maximum fare anyway whether first- or second-class, so it made no odds except for my fare. There was less likely to be a crowded carriage.

I had forgotten about food and dogs. No diner will take dogs and there was no buffet. At Euston we had trouble with the electric wagons the porters drive, and I battled with a panicky dog and my holdall, wondering if I would be in time to see my father.

I asked a waitress at the Euston buffet if she could bring sandwiches and coffee to the door. No. She was busy and I shouldn't travel with a dog.

I bought a couple of bananas at the kiosk and struggled with the coffee machine. Another passenger came to my rescue and held Janus for me. He had a Golden Retriever at home. We talked dogs. He had a train to catch or he would have held the dog while I queued for a sandwich.

I took a taxi, knowing we could never cope with the Tube or buses.

Suppose the taxi driver objected to dogs?

He grinned as we got in. He had a Labrador. I asked if we would find a square with trees. Where was I going? Victoria. We could do better than that. We could have a run in the park and he wouldn't set the meter till afterwards.

The ticket collector at Victoria was extremely offensive about rich women travelling first-class taking their dogs on holiday. In November! The money I had spent on the dog alone would feed a family for a week. He elaborated. I wished I were a witch and could turn him into a toad. I was far too miserable to say anything at all. People were looking at us; Janus was dragging me, and I felt exhausted.

The train journey was endless, but we arrived at last and I went to the hospital. I stayed four days, until the ward sister said it was pointless to stay on; my sister was with my mother and there was nothing more I could do.

I went home. Christmas, which was not far away, was going to be bleak. Dad had said, 'See you at Christmas,' and I had said 'of course', knowing there could be no Christmas for him.

The same ticket collector was on duty, loathing me on sight again, asking if the dog had had a good holiday and only the best steak. I could cheerfully have strangled him, but again there was no use saying anything. He would almost certainly not have believed me.

This time I called in at my agent's; she had coffee and sandwiches ready, and a drink for Janus; a little while to talk about things that didn't matter very much and then go home.

Somewhere on that journey realisation hit me and I didn't hear the guard when he spoke to me.

'Are you all right?' he asked. He was an elderly man, with a kind face. I told him about my father.

He clipped the ticket without another word. Twenty

minutes later he came back with coffee and sandwiches, which he sat and watched me eat, refusing to take a penny for them, talking about his grandchildren, stroking the dog, leaving briefly to go about his duties and then coming back again. There was no one else in the compartment.

At Stockport he returned to hold Janus while I got off the train.

I doubt if I would recognise him again but I will never forget him.

My brother rang next morning with the news we had been dreading.

Life went on.

Puma made slow progress and then quite suddenly a corner was turned. She and Pan began to recover and came about with me again. Judy was by now up and on crutches, which at first the dogs hated, but they soon grew used to them. She was able to go out to the kennels and supervise, and arrange for bitches to be mated again. By the time the first of them whelped she was mobile and able to cope. She always stays with the bitch during the whole of the birth, day or night, to ensure everything is in order. So she has to be fit.

The pups had had lead poisoning at a most unfortunate time in their lives. They should have been going out and about; should have been meeting people, learning to be total extroverts. Instead they had been shut away in the dark for nearly eleven weeks, and only seen Marian and Sheila, with the vet, as an unwanted bonus, sticking needles into them.

But the pups had survived.

I took Puma to Knutsford on market day, plunging her in at the deep end. I was doubtful when Judy suggested it, as I knew what Janus had been like when he first saw traffic. Judy thought this would be different as the pups had spent the first sixteen weeks of their lives in the

103

whelping kennel, which was free from oncoming litters, owing to Judy's leg, which proved, peculiarly, to have been a blessing in one way.

Had there been more pups, they would have been removed from that run much earlier. Also, Puma had often been out with me.

Janus had spent his first weeks in a place where traffic was never seen; except for some brief experience involving a milk float.

Puma, on the contrary, spent her first weeks in a run that has been built, deliberately, in a busy part of the farmyard, right beside the kennel kitchen where the dog food is mixed. There are horses at livery; their owners come to and fro in cars to exercise them, the cars reversing beside the puppy run, being parked outside it, within sniffing distance, while the horses are saddled in the yard, and canter off along the run.

There are cattle in the field on the other side of the run; there are trees nearby, so the wind in the trees is a constant sound from the time the pups begin to hear.

There is no creeping about. Horse hooves clatter; the delivery lorries, some of them, especially that bringing puppy and dog food, enormous, come into the yard, and reverse within feet of the kennel. Engines rev. Men shout. Dustbins clatter. The pups are used to the din from the start of their lives, and come out into a busy scene that fascinates them.

Everyone coming to the farm goes up to the puppy run. No one can resist those tumbling black and gold bundles squealing for attention. They stand up against the wire to have their tummies tickled, sniff hands, and watch the big dogs let out for exercise, running in a pack past the run.

Judy's Alsatian pack was one of our delights. Sheila took out the dogs five or six at a time. The stud dog, Shah, Puma's grandfather (who became a champion when Puma was two years old, and sadly, had to be put to sleep because

104

of a brain tumour recently) let out his bitches, keeping them in order, never allowing any of them to get the upper hand of him. He was boss.

Once in the big field, the dogs ran, stretching their legs, vying with one another to be first, a long loping gallop, in a pack, that was wonderful to watch. When the big dogs had exercised, the young stock went out. No stud dogs are ever allowed together as they fight, jealousy of one another making certain that the fights are fierce and very dangerous, so that not even Shah's sons went out with him once they had had a bitch of their own. That was the turning point.

The young stock raced and played and tumbled, sometimes in the big field by themselves, sometimes in the second field with the horses; Belinda's gelding, that had come to her too lame to race any more, and been nursed, until he was well enough to hack and hunt; Stephen's little grey pony, Razzle, a character all his own; Judy's chestnut; Jane's pretty mare, who was also stabled there; dogs and horses ran together and when the half-Arab mares were bought and had their foals, they ran too. Judy and I took time off to watch at the gate, and laugh as the pups tumbled over, trying to keep up.

When Janus was fit he ran with the young stock, ambling happily after them, unable to match their pace, and sidetracked by the delicious smells on the ground. Rabbit and mole; weasel and stoat, and pheasants. There was a keepered wood on one side of Judy's land, and at Christmas a syndicate shot there which resulted that year in a minor tragedy as somebody with bad eyesight mistook Stephen's ginger cat for a rabbit, and poor Ginger was found shot dead just before Christmas dinner was served. Everyone was fond of the cat. It didn't make for a happy Christmas and there was further worry in case an even worse shot hit one of the dogs by accident. They didn't seem to be very skilful.

105

On fresh sunny days the dogs went with Sheila to the river, which is clean and fresh, and as yet unpolluted, and romped in the shallow water, enjoying every minute. By spring Judy was able to take them herself, and resume one of her major pleasures. She also began to ride again, though that was painful as her leg was unused to exercise.

So although Puma had been shut away, her first days had been packed with experience and Judy hoped this would have patterned her ready for life outside. Judy was right. I could not take Janus out into the town on market day; he was a shivering wreck and it was far too exhausting, but Puma leaped out, eager to see the fun.

She walked beside me beautifully. She has never been a puller, and had to be taught to thrust out when in the Breed ring, and run ahead of her handler. She loved it, her head coming up to look at me, her ears moving to catch every sound. She watched the cattle trucks with interest, quite unbothered by them. She never flinched when the milk tanker passed us in the lane, and we had to lean into the hedge, as there is no pavement, whereas Janus had to be reassured or he would have bolted.

She loved the shops. She paused, staring in at the window displays, fascinated. In order to get her more accustomed to strange places, I took her into the pet shop, where dogs are welcomed, and where she rapidly made a big impression. She was a most beautiful pup, with a lovely lean body, and excellent shape. Also she has a very pretty head, and her puppy face was enchanting.

People stopped to pet her, and she revelled in their attention. From then on, the busy town was part of our weekly routine, and although I was still visiting my mother as often as was possible, I had more time to spare for Puma. Petrol in those days was still cheap; the eleven mile journey made a very small dent in my budget, and enabled me to walk Janus where it was quiet, and life was less harassing.

The pups, in the normal way, would have entered puppy classes at six-months-old, but these two were ill then. Judy eyed Puma whenever she saw her, becoming more and more convinced that she was indeed the pick of the litter, and should be shown.

Even I, without, as yet, an eye for Alsatians, could see her quality, though I was not at all sure that wasn't personal bias. But I knew Janus was far from a show specimen; he has a poor rib cage, a very poor coat, his body is too long, and his gait is terrible. But he has a glorious head and lovely paws and it doesn't make the slightest odds to me; his character redeems all his show faults and I had never intended to show him anyway.

I agreed that while Puma was with Judy, she should take her to shows with her own stock. Eric was to handle her; the Alsatian ring is a marathon and it is not easy for most people to stride out fast enough to show off the pace of a really good animal. I do handle Puma myself now in local shows, but I can't give her the advantage she needs, as she restricts her speed to mine, which spoils her movement.

We watched Puma move. She has a wonderful action, covering the ground effortlessly, her head up, her eyes alight with enjoyment, speeding fast. Janus races after her, every movement of his body anxiously saying 'wait for me', and then she turns and comes back to him and they play together in mock battle, apparently eating one another's ears.

They growl in mock fury, often worrying strangers who are convinced they are fighting, but I know the fighting tone, and it is nothing like that.

Judy and Eric assured me Puma was special; she had something lacking in other dogs and she also had a show presence. I thought they were trying to cheer me up and expected absolutely nothing from her, especially in a first

107

show. Also her first outing, contrary to the usual custom, was to be at a championship show, where the top dogs go, and not a little show to give her experience, where the competition is less daunting.

I didn't realise just what a championship show meant. Dog shows had never been part of my life; though my neighbours showed their two English setters I had always thought it a bit of a game, like a beauty queen show, or a baby show. It is, in some ways, but it has a much more valid purpose, as I soon learned.

Shows are the shop windows for the top breeders. If a kennel can produce dogs that win regularly in the ring, then they are reported in the dog papers, and the kennel names are noticed. I hadn't realised until I read that first show catalogue, that Judy had sold so many animals that were making a mark; and so had Jess. Velindre Gorsefield cropped up again and again, together or alone.

Puma was to enter the Bolton and District Alsatian Club championship show on January 27th 1973. It was her first show ever. I wasn't able to go. I didn't expect her to be placed, as she had missed so much of her puppyhood, and was unable to compete with the young pups; she had to go in with older pups that were already experienced in the shows. Some of them are veterans in show experience by the time they are nine months old.

Judy rang me that evening.

Puma had come second in her class, which was a strong class of excellent animals, and the competition had been fierce. She was delighted. I was astounded. Puma was quite unknown, and had moved straight up among the pups of whom future wins were expected.

My championship card came to me next time I went to walk my little bitch, along with her prize money of £1. Prize money in the dog world is very little; there are few sponsored shows, and expenses are heavy. The card and the rosette mean far more than the money; no one enters dog showing to make a fortune.

I was still too tied up to get to the shows. Puma was fourth in the Southern Alsatian Training Society Championship show on March 10th, again travelling with Eric and some of Judy's older dogs, with Sheila to look after them on the benches and prepare them for their classes, grooming them till their coats shone.

That is never difficult with Puma who has a gleaming coat that needs very little attention.

It was soon to be my mother's birthday and my brother and his wife and I were clubbing together to give her a West Highland White terrier. Judy helped us find a reliable breeder, and the puppy was chosen and booked, to be handed over when my mother came to visit at Easter. She began to look forward to something again and prepare for the pup, and all her letters now were about the Westie, which she had already named Lucky.

On March 17th, Puma was entered for the North Wales Alsatian Club Open Show. I was busy with a book, Janus, unbelievably improved in health, was obviously no longer likely to be put down, and I had a problem, as I now had two dogs, and I had no desire at all to sell Puma. Not only was she a delight in herself, greeting me with fervour whenever I came out, as the source of more fun than kennels, but I was fascinated by her show potential and I was realising that my old ambition that had been so laughed at, to have a brood bitch and breed pups, was within an ace of coming true.

'She's a lovely bitch, Joyce,' Judy said, every time she saw me.

Her judges loved her, and I began to learn that dog jargon is different from everyday language, and as in all walks of life, is quite specialised.

One of Puma's show write-ups said, 'This flashy bitch moves beautifully.'

To my uneducated mind, a flashy bitch was a most

109

derogatory remark and I was indignant. We were lunching in the Chapel and Judy and Eric were both reduced to laughter and unable to explain. Belinda, Judy's daughter, explained that in dog jargon a 'flashy bitch' was high praise indeed, and meant she had a lovely rich colouring.

I was still unable to believe that Puma had potential although I found her gorgeous. In spite of the lead poisoning she had recovered all her gaiety and every time I went out to Judy's there was a new saga about my puppy, usually referred to now by Les as 'Joyce's damned little bitch'.

It was Puma who made off with Les's best shoes, and left one down the horse field, and buried the other in the midden. It was Puma who was delighted to see a tub full of marigolds put there for her express benefit. In no time at all the tub was empty and the marigolds were all over the yard.

She was now separated from Panther, as she was liable to fight him for his food, and win. They were kennelled separately, Puma having her own run and bench inside the big barn that had been the original cause of all the trouble. Les had burned off all the paint, right down to the raw wood, and repainted everywhere, taking immense care the new paint had no trace of lead.

Panther was very excitable; Puma only excitable when someone came to relieve her boredom with food or walks, and she was beginning to know the show routine; the grooming, the cleaning up, as kennelled dogs get very mucky, and then the ride in Eric's van and the smell and savour of the show venue, and all the dogs.

Her head went up as soon as she arrived, and she behaved as if the whole affair had been put on for her express benefit. In the ring, she shone, with a star quality that at that North Wales show won her the Algarry cup for the Best Puppy. It stood on my bookcase for a whole year, amusing those who looked at it, as the plaque announced

110

that it was to be held for a year, unless won three times running by the same dog or bitch. But what dog or bitch remains a pup for three years? They were safe enough with that one. With it came a little shield with an Alsatian head on it, that stands with Puma's trophies.

The dogs that year began to give me far more satisfaction. Janus improved beyond recognition, so much so that Dot, a friend of Marian's, coming on a visit to Parr's Wood training class, which I now attended as Marian taught there, looked at the dog and fussed him, and then a little diffidently said, 'Joyce, what happened to Janus? Did you have to have him put to sleep?'

'That *is* Janus,' I said.

She found it hard to believe. It was six months since she had seen him; greyhound thin, every rib sticking out, gaunt faced, and wildly excitable. And here he was well up to normal retriever weight, as he had gained two pounds a week for ten weeks and then levelled out once he began to absorb his food properly. My vet put him on extra vitamins. I hadn't realised how much his coat had improved.

Also now he was feeling fitter, he was responding to training, and far more biddable. He greeted Dot gaily, worked on the floor, and every time I sat down she said, 'I can't believe it.'

We were all beginning to pick ourselves up again. Judy had a new litter at the kennels, and I saw the pups when I went out to Puma. One day she too would have pups. I looked forward to that immensely. But not until she was two years old as Judy doesn't believe in pushing a young bitch. Her bones aren't set and carrying the litter is far too much of a strain. Also the pups take calcium from her that she needs to firm her own body.

Puma entered Manchester Championship show at Belle Vue. I was able to get to that as it is only five miles away. The competition is very high indeed as it is the second

111

biggest and most important show after Cruft's. Puma came seventh, which both Judy and Eric felt good under the circumstances. I had to go home at lunch time and see to Janus, as his tummy was not yet completely under control and he needed to go out more often than a normal dog. Also, while we were stabilising him, so that he could digest his food, he had three meals a day instead of one.

We added Heinz baby beef dinner to each meal, introducing it to him gradually, as that is pre-digested, and the change in him was so rapid that even I could see it happening and the people at Wilmslow Road who had criticised me were fascinated. He was a different dog in every way, except that he still preferred to play the fool rather than work when we were on the floor.

And he was far too interested in bitches.

At Liverpool Alsatian Club Open show on April 7th, Puma was Best Puppy, with another cup to add to our trophies and another shield, and a lovely big rosette. I began to try and make time to go with her, which wasn't at all easy, as I was so busy at home. The weeks were never long enough and in the winter Kenneth was home for weekends, and we rarely saw one another apart from that. He was as interested in dog shows as I was in boating. But once the boat went back in the water I would be free at weekends, and then could start show going.

Puma had a fourth at Haydock Park; and another second at the Bolton Alsatian club championship show, and then came the first show I was free to attend near Crewe, at a lovely venue at Doddington Hall, an old mansion in a park. It was a fine sunny day, everyone was relaxed and there were Alsatians everywhere.

Janus couldn't come into the show, but it was out of doors, and the car park, Judy told me, was under trees. I could leave him there and commute to him and give him

1. *A dual purpose lesson. Janus is being taught not to touch my little seal ornament, which he liked to steal. And simultaneously the kittens are being taught that the dog is harmless.*

2. *Chia (on the left) and Casey, when grown, loved to sit on the windowsill and watch intently while the dog was taught, so that they could share his reward of a minute piece of hard cheese.*

3. *The culmination of one childhood ambition. By now the pups were old enough to sell and Puma weary of maternity. The pup standing on her tail is Gorsefield Balta, her son, now at stud and winning first prizes himself at the shows.*

4. *When visitors come with young children the dogs are penned unless I am free to supervise all the time. A large dog, getting excited, might knock over a small child. And children unused to dogs may harm or tease and provoke a major incident. The pen is a bore, but it's better to be safe than sorry where dogs are concerned.*

5. *Training sessions are much easier if the dogs are first played with and are alert and excited. A bored dog won't learn. So before every session there is a game to make them interested. They can't wait to come and see.*

6. My favourite training aid for both these dogs is a toy that squeaks; the sound calls them in, acts as a signal, and alerts their attention. Puma here is only just beginning to learn what squeaking is about; Janus knows, and is anxious to have his turn too.

7. Serious training begins; all the dog's concentration on the toy in my hand, so that other distractions are ignored. It keeps him close in and working well.

8. *Retrievers are born to retrieve and Janus will try anything, but the broom proved difficult until he found it easier to carry in mid handle, when it balanced well.*

9. *At one time Janus had a habit of dropping his dumbbell instead of giving it to me; this exercise practises holding until commanded to release the bell, and cures a bad habit.*

10. *German Shepherds are not bred for retrieving, but for guarding. Puma hated holding anything in her mouth until I taught her to carry the dish the cats had just fed from. It smelled of meat, and now she too will retrieve happily. There's always a way out of a problem with dogs.*

11. *I hope one day to teach Puma agility and tracking; this is the very beginning exercise, over a low jump that is gradually raised until she can do the show height. The increase is gentle, and the dog is unaware of the differences.*

12. *Scent is one of the more difficult exercises. Here Janus is being given the scent from my hand, which is also on one of the cloths. The others, which I had not touched, were put out by the photographer. He has to find my scented cloth and bring it in to me.*

13. *Those who think it cruel to train a dog to be sensible should think again, and look at this picture. Both dogs know that lessons are about to begin and are waiting eagerly to see which of them is to be first. Janus hopes that his SIT without a command will influence me to start with him!*

14. The dogs that were initially my despair were both trainable. Puma has not yet won in Obedience though she has come near it; in Breed she does very well and here shows off her prizes. Janus too has his share, won in various Obedience shows, and he too has had two cups to prove his prowess.

water and exercise and just before Puma's class I romped the two dogs together outside the grounds.

Puma won her class, and then, when competing with the pup that won the first puppy class, came Best Puppy Bitch and I had a big rosette to take home with me to add to her growing number of trophies. I had one of Kenneth's old ties to pin them on, hung in a corner of the dining room, to give me a lift when life was on one of its down movements. We seemed to go up and down like yo-yos at that time.

But at least the dogs were fit.

Janus was posing one minor problem in that I couldn't take him into shows when I took Puma; and I couldn't leave him at home alone all day as he needed to go out midday. He could now have two meals a day; and if we were travelling, no longer lost condition visibly if he went back to one. There was no one to leave with him at home, now Dorothy had retired. Her family were grown up and away from home, and she wanted freedom to visit them.

It was then that someone suggested I started Janus in Obedience shows; I could enter him where there was Breed and Obedience and take him in. I don't like leaving dogs in cars in icy weather or very hot weather; and often we did not know until we arrived what kind of parking facilities were available. At some shows there is only the town car park, some way from the venue and there are problems getting in again if you leave the show. Also you can't take out a dog that has been entered for competition, even for a few minutes, but have to find someone to hold it if there is no benching.

Janus knew the obedience routine; he wasn't good; he was nowhere near show standard; and I wasn't going to impress the judges. But I did want to take Puma myself; it was one of my few chances to be with her all day. When I picked her up I sometimes had Judy as passenger and a couple of other dogs as well. It's surprising how much you can pack into a Mini. Mine was permanently converted into a dog carrier, with the wire guard behind the driver's seat, so there was plenty of room in the rear for several dogs, as it was the Estate version.

Puma had another show with Eric, travelling to Glasgow on my birthday, May 26th. She was entered in two classes, having won her way out of the puppy classes. There are rules which govern the entries and a winning dog cannot compete in any class after winning that class twice when young. Though if entered at another show before the second win, it is possible to win several on the trot.

Puma had won her two Puppy Firsts and a third as bonus, having entered well before the closing date, and not won her second First until after the closing date of the third show. She could now no longer enter Puppy classes. That meant that at only a year old, she had to go up among older bitches, into the Maiden class.

'No problem,' said Eric, using one of his favourite phrases. 'Puma can do it. What's more, she could do Novice as well. You might as well enter her in both classes at each show. If she does enough winning, she could get a Junior Warrant.'

It was the first time I had heard of the award. Eric explained.

A dog or bitch earns a Junior Warrant, which is a kind of junior championship award, if it gains twenty-five points in shows before the age of eighteen months. It is an award that breeders covet and it is not easy to gain. A First in an Open show counts as one point. A First in a championship show counts as three points. Puma had a number of points already, as the day before Eric proposed this she had come first in her Maiden class at the Birmingham championship show. She had six months in which she could gain the remaining nineteen points. It seemed like one of those dreams, and I was sure she wouldn't do it.

Eric was full of confidence; Judy hedged her bets. 'Well,

she might.' But now we had real competition as two bitches in particular were her major rivals. Wauchopes Francesca and Gailsmoor Carousel who Judy thought the loveliest bitches she had ever seen at the time. I preferred my Puma, obviously, but once I had seen Carousel and Francesca I knew we had tough competition and also suspected, being rational, that Puma was outclassed in every way. They are both gorgeous.

By now I was able to go to most of the shows. The first thing Judy and I did was to look up the catalogue and see if our two rivals were entered. If not we could be pretty sure of a winning point; if they were, it all depended on how they showed and how Puma showed. Francesca had a very long journey to most shows as she came from Scotland. Sometimes she was obviously journey stale when she came into the ring.

But I knew Puma had no chance in Glasgow as there Francesca was right on her own doorstep, and she was certain to be entered. Puma was in two classes that day; Maiden and Novice. She could get six more points. But not with that competition.

We celebrated my birthday, and I was just about to go to bed, expecting nothing, when Eric rang.

'A double First,' he said. 'Puma won both her classes. Six more points to her Junior Warrant. I told you she'd make it.'

I bought him a silver goblet to celebrate. Puma greeted me gaily on the Monday when I went out. I rarely went to Mobberley at weekends as the kennels was so busy and Les was home, working around the place, and it seemed unfair to interrupt them. Someone always had to fetch Puma for me, as otherwise I disturbed all the other dogs in the kennel block as they didn't know me, and barked.

It was getting harder and harder to leave her, especially as Judy said she was a very affectionate little bitch and deprived in kennels; she was the wrong type. Hard dogs don't mind lack of human companionship. Puma did. She always exploded towards me, doing a seal wriggle, like her mother, Witch, smiling up at me; she greeted everyone in the same way. I wasn't special. I was just someone else to take her around and give her fun, ranking a long way down the line from Sheila and Marian who had fed her as a pup and still fed her; and Sheila took her out in the fields and down to the river, and Eric took her to shows. It wasn't any way to start a dog I hoped would one day be mine completely.

But I was still going to Bexhill quite often; and it seemed mean to bring Puma to my house and then have to kennel her as I certainly couldn't travel at that time with two dogs. Puma wasn't house-trained. Janus was by now far easier to travel with and was angelic in the car, curling up in the well of the passenger seat, lying there all the time the car was in motion, putting his nose on my knee if I stopped for a drink from my Thermos flask, knowing the routine very well.

We walked in quiet woods beside laybys, and though he was still liable to lunge after a rabbit smell, he was easier to handle.

So maybe it would be a good idea to take him to a show and see how he fared. There was an Open show with Breed and Obedience. I could enter Janus in the Beginners class, and have him with me while Puma entered her Breed class.

I should have known Janus.

He was an absolute fiend from the word Go. He wasn't panicky. He was once more wildly excited, this time about bitches. Bitches galore. Some newly out of season; some about to come into season and one or two actually in season, all smothered in anti-mate which doesn't fool any dog.

No in-season bitch is allowed in Obedience; but they

116

appear to be allowed in Breed, as the rules merely state that mating is not allowed within the show precincts and some breeders will bring stud dog and bitch together after the show, at some point on the homeward journey, to save extra travelling.

The result is that those of us with highly-sexed dogs or stud dogs in Obedience might as well not bother to compete. I travelled the Bisto kid with me; Janus had on his most eager and appealing expression, his nose in the air, his eyes half closed, an expression of total bliss on his face.

He smelled bitch as soon as he got out of the car. He nearly pulled me over. Judy, having bred Alsatians for as long as I've been writing, laughed at my incompetence, and said, 'Joyce, give him to me.'

Confident that she could handle anything, she took him. He nearly pulled her over. After a few minutes she handed him back saying that he was a devil and she'd never known a dog like him. Alsatians don't behave like that.

She has since had cause to change her mind, but up to that day she hadn't met Puma's son.

It was a disastrous day. Everywhere we went, there were bitches. Janus darted from one to the other. He became so excited he didn't care if it were dog or bitch, and by the end of the day at least twelve people had offered to kill my dog, including Sheila who had been an object of his attentions too, much to her horror. Her fierce reaction merely startled Janus. It didn't change his mind.

He thought one Alsatian dog was a bitch.

There was a fight.

He was leashed and it was stopped at once, but by now I was sick of him. He always let me down in public, yet in private he was perfect. He could win Cruft's at home. Here, he only won disapproval and he misbehaved so evilly, with a wicked grin on his face, savouring every ecstatic moment.

Work in the ring was disastrous. Any resemblance to

what he should have done was purely coincidental, probably due to a bitch walking in front of him, alongside the ring, in the direction we were going. At every corner he veered towards the bitch ring, which was far too close to us for comfort.

Someone offered to operate on him with two bricks.

A few days later in the Chapel Inn, I told David, who had come up to see to one of the horses, and joined us for our usual baked bean toastie and a drink. He wasn't at all sure about neutering the dog, but Judy was.

'If you don't do it, I probably will,' she said.

Eric's guard dog, Zimba, had been neutered some years before for the same reason. Though people said neutering fattened dogs, Zimba is hard and lean and fit, and enjoys life immensely. Val, Head Trainer at Wilmslow, had also had Prince, her retired Labrador, neutered many years before, and Prince too was hard and fit and obviously hadn't suffered. I had no doubts, as I knew both dogs well. Val thought it might help calm Janus.

Janus *was* neutered and while under the anaesthetic he was X-rayed for his hips. The X-rays shows his left hip socket is non-existent; it is almost straight and the bone head is above it, barely touching. The bone might have slipped out of the socket the night he screamed. We will never know. We have always kept his weight to the minimum desirable for a dog of his size on the vet's recommendation. Too much weight could cause the hip to collapse completely. He is not allowed titbits.

Janus, of course had his own ideas about the way a dog should recover from an operation. He was discommoded for precisely six hours, and then he became very interested in the stitch ends protruding from his tummy, and began to chew them.

I took him back to the vet with one stitch teased out and the others looking angry. He was tidied up, a process he accepted with his usual philosophical stoicism. No matter

118

what was done to him, he always went up to David afterwards, putting his head against his hand, or offering his paw. Janus has never been afraid of any vet, probably because our first one, who we had to leave because of distance when David put his plate up, went to immense trouble to reassure a frightened little dog, talking to him, stroking him, and generally trying to make the experience as unfrightening as possible. David does the same. So does my new vet, as we have now moved home.

'He'll have to wear a weaning jacket,' David said. Bitches wear these, to prevent the pups suckling from them while they are being weaned.

I made a weaning jacket, from an old sheet. Janus looked absurd and knew it. He cavorted around, being as ridiculous as he knew how, then rolled over and tore it off him and started up on the stitches again.

I told Celia, my next-door-neighbour, who had recently moved in, and who had a lovely Border collie, Moss, at that time. Poor Moss was chasing a stick some months later, that penetrated his throat, killing him. We have never used sticks as playthings since.

Celia suggested rolled cheesecloth, which comes in sausage shapes, that her son used to clean up his motor bike. We managed to get Janus into it, in a hysterical session that wasn't helped by the fact that Janus loved being laughed at, so that he pranced and cavorted and grinned at us, and rolled over and bicycled, looking as absurd as any dog could do, covered in cheesecloth.

His operation did not inconvenience him at all. We went out as usual, went over to Puma, producing gales of laughter at the kennels when Janus appeared in his jacket, which he had to wear in the car, though we took it off to walk him. Getting him in and out was a bit like trying to put sausage meat into too small a skin and took a remarkable amount of time, especially as I never could do it without laughing at him, which immediately turned on his sense of fun, and he became a prancing nutcase, with his tail fanning my face.

He enjoyed visiting Judy too. I often lunched there now, and walked Puma, Panther, and Janus together. Janus had steadied enough for this to be possible, and slowly the fact that neither Puma nor Pan worried about vehicles gave him confidence. He hated the milk tanker when it came close; I was never sure whether his fear came from the vehicle, or was associated with the smell of milk. But he accepted other vehicles more philosophically, though he still has, even now, to turn round and identify a new kind of moving object. He watches it thoughtfully, always close against my leg, but he no longer tries to bolt.

Visits to Judy meant racing in the meadow. It was good for Janus to be with other dogs, though we did have one occasion that worried us.

Janus had been attacked several times by other dogs. He showed no sign of aggression and did not attempt to defend himself. Even when attacked by the dog he had tried to mate with at Bolton, he had merely barked, I thought in astonishment, but had not attempted to fight properly. It might be easier if he defended himself and discouraged his attackers.

Eric suggested Janus played with Zorra, his young long-haired Alsatian, who plays rough. We ran the two dogs together; Zorra plays by mock battle all the time, and after five or six attempts, Janus suddenly retaliated.

It wasn't a good idea, as when put with Panther and Klaus in the field next day, he attacked both of them, positive this was what dogs did. We had to break up the fight and run Janus and Puma alone, and that was the end of socialising with the dogs. He was safe enough with the bitches and if he got enthusiastic with older bitches, they warned him off in no uncertain terms and he learned to leave them alone.

Judy had a number of animals at this time, among them

120

store cattle and livery horses as well as the family horses and her brood mares and their foals. There were also more than twenty dogs, of several breeds. The horses and cattle accepted Alsatians, but they were all very suspicious of the golden dog that came occasionally to the field, and we had to watch them. Janus seemed unaware of their possible animosity. He trusted everything and was much too curious.

Judy's brood bitches didn't like him either as he had to pass the puppy kennel to get into the field, and though they never bothered if an Alsatian ran past, they made a good deal of noise about him. After one tentative sniff at one lot of puppies, he never went close again, as Mum came racing at him, meaning business. It was a good job there was stout wire between them.

That summer Judy and I spent a lot of time on the lawn with puppies running between us. One litter in particular were extremely funny as they were very vocal. There were four of them. Judy, like all good breeders, knows that early human handling makes a lot of difference to their future relationship with humans, so that they are encouraged to come out and clamber over us, as we kneel on the grass.

These pups ran between us, squealing up at us, as if telling us a great deal; and then rushed over to the other human, to clamber into a lap and sit there, small faces looking up, declaiming busily. Janus and Puma watched from the car.

I was learning a good deal more about dogs and about shows.

And a good deal more about Judy, and about breeders, and about pedigree Alsatians. The names of famous kennels were no longer a mystery to me and I was beginning to associate faces with the kennel names; they weren't just names in a book. I had met Francesca's owners, John and Betty Gribben, and we were very friendly rivals. I haven't, even yet, met Carousel's owners.

121

More and more, our thoughts were on that Junior Warrant, which we had to get before Puma was eighteen months old, in November. Often it turns into a cliffhanger, a week to go and a point needed, a point that remains elusive, as if the judges knew you were praying for it and were determined to foil you.

It isn't like that, of course, but sometimes it seems as if it must be.

We spent time poring over show schedules, discussing judges, and distances and dates. I found it all new and fascinating and Judy is an excellent teacher.

Chapter 8

I was trying to learn as much as I could about breeding. I had already learned some things from my experience with Janus. I knew too that it is far from simple to ensure every litter is one hundred per cent perfect. Accidents happen in the best of kennels. Judy had one pup born with too small a heart. Emma was gorgeous, but had several odd 'turns' that the vet couldn't account for, until she was X-rayed and the truth was revealed. It was just one of those things, and not hereditary. Judy was running Klaus on to succeed Emma when she died; but Emma managed to survive and live a happy life and her owner was willing to keep her as she was. Apart from being unable to take a great deal of exercise, she lived an absolutely normal life, and when I last saw her was a very happy dog.

We were no longer able to enter Puma in the Maiden class, as she had won her way out of that, and now was entered in Novice and in Junior. The class names have all been changed since then; some remain but there are new names for old classes and I still get confused, as among the new names are Graduate and Postgraduate which are self-evident as to order, but then there are Limit classes, sometimes Limit and Mid Limit and I always have to look them up to see which we can now enter.

At Leeds at a championship show, Puma came fourth, and second, so no points were added towards her warrant. At Chester she was fifth in both her classes; again no points. You can never tell where a dog will come, as the competition varies. Some shows may bring out a mass of splendid stock; others may bring none, and there are judges who nobody in the know will enter under. A new judge is learning, and may not yet be knowledgeable enough, and make mistakes in the placings. Some judges do show prejudice, and may go for colour, putting up all sables, or all blacks, and ignoring the others. If you have a judge that prefers a hard black German type of bitch, well up to the standard size, it is no use putting Puma, who is dainty, and black and gold, with a gold face, under her or him, and if the fees are high to enter and the travelling is distant, then we don't bother.

A lot of it is luck; who is there on your day; and how your dog shows.

Occasionally one suspects malpractice, but it's very rare; there are too many other judges watching at the ringside, who know the ropes and what goes on, and you aren't asked to judge again if people complain too often.

We were considering stud dogs already, although Puma was not to be mated until next year. It takes time to sort them out, as we not only wanted to know what the dog was like, but we wanted to see his progeny. He might be gorgeous, but not every gorgeous dog produces good pups. And above all, with the Alsatian, we wanted good temperament, which is absolutely vital in that breed. It is in all breeds; there are goldies about that should never have been bred, and a line of Labradors coming from somewhere that are horrors; some Cockers can be utterly foul; so it isn't just the Alsatian. But no breed is bad all through and none is perfect, so you must shop around, and we intended to do a lot of research before mating Puma, as Judy does with all her bitches. She is also particular about accepting bitches sfor her stud dogs, as not all make good matches, and if the pups are bad the dog may be blamed even if it is a fault that has come through the bitch.

We had blood tests done on Puma to make sure there was no hangover from the lead poisoning. They were quite normal. So was she, in every way. She loved shows and walks and living generally and she was becoming attached to Janus. She saw a great deal of him, and travelled with him in the car.

He in his turn loved going to see her, becoming eager and excited as soon as we turned into the lane, sitting up expectantly, head up, ears cocked, watching for Puma to come out of her kennel, greeting her delightedly. She always licked his face when they met. He butted her, and they lay side by side, chewing one another's ears, apparently gaining great pleasure from the act.

Going to a show with Puma was another delight. Janus knew as soon as his wooden dumbbell for the retrieve in ring came into the car that we were off to fetch her. He couldn't have enough of her; another dog to play with, all the time. They travelled perfectly together, both lying still while the car was moving, and it was a familiar routine.

At the shows, Judy joined me part of the time, looking at dog after dog. Was he sound? Did he move well? What was his pedigree? No, not that; it's too close to Puma, and I don't want those lines on both sides; not that one; I saw his last litter; they're all very nervous. Not that one; he has the same fault as Puma; his feet aren't too good, and we need to counteract her feet, which are her worst point. She has long toes and enormous claws that need constant cutting, but the quick is near the end, so they cannot be cut very short.

Not that dog. He has one of the ancestors that Nem Elliott mentioned in her book, *Modern Bloodlines in the Alsatian*. It carries epilepsy; the last thing we want. German

125

Shepherd breeders are lucky in that there are books available warning them of faults that can arise so that they can avoid the strains that carry major weaknesses. Only some don't bother and some are ostriches and won't allow a breath of their faults to get out; there are slip ups; sometimes the totally innocent can suffer, as the owner of a stud dog has kept his faults very dark indeed. But the vast majority of breeders do care a great deal. There is now an Improvement Society that is trying to bring all faults out into the open so that breeders can get together and strengthen the breed.

By now I also knew a good deal about Judy.

Go to a show. 'What's the competition, Joyce, have you looked?' And then we turn to Puma's class. 'She won't come higher than third today. You haven't seen that bitch have you? Watch out for her. She's glorious. I'd put her first today if I were judging.' Judy does judge, and judges championship shows. She had judged in South Africa and been asked to go to New Zealand. Her classes are always enormous and so are Jess Moore's, as both of them are passionate about the breed, and put up the dog that is best without fear or favour. And people value their opinions.

There was never envy when she spoke. Only total admiration and a completely professional, objective look, aware of the faults in her own stock as well as those in others. Puma isn't perfect; no animal ever is.

I began to realise Puma had more potential than I thought when I started to watch out for Francesca and Carousel. They vied with one another, and she was as much a threat to them as they to her. Their results were rarely predictable. Puma could come first, second, or third against them, a lot of it depending on how they all looked on the day of the show.

Francesca had that very long journey, starting out at three in the morning for shows which to us were local;

126

Puma, we discovered, had seasons every seventeen weeks, and during them she was off colour, and after them she was worse. We couldn't understand why. She became a miserable plodder, showing very badly.

Yet, even like that, she could come fourth or fifth in a big class. But I had given up hope of her Junior Warrant. She just wasn't shining any more. Everyone began to ask what was happening to Puma and tell me how often the sparkling puppy became a stolid animal with no go in it, that failed to win.

She had come into season just after Glasgow show so perhaps that accounted for her next failures. I hadn't much hope for her when she went with Eric to the Three Counties show at Malvern, another at which Championships Certificates were given. They aren't given at Open shows or any of the smaller ones, and many breeders, with costs that are high, only enter the Championship shows, once they have accustomed the dog to showing.

Much to my pleasure, she came first in her novice class and second in the Junior class, which was much stronger. Eric was pleased, and Judy was delighted as that was three more points towards the warrant and we still had six months to play with. She had fifteen points. She needed ten more.

We went to all the shows we could. Janus came too, working after a fashion. His show record was horrid. I was totally ashamed of us. But Puma made up for it, though a lot of Obedience people think Breed showing is ridiculous and a lot of Breed people think Obedience absurd. I think there is a place for both; and would like to see more breeders try for dual Breed/Obedience champions as a trained dog is so much easier to handle and it's good for the dogs to use their brains. Many breed dogs never get the chance as they are kennel kept and know as little as a child that never comes out of one room at the top of a high-rise block of flats. No dog can gain experience shut up for hours every day.

Blackpool Championship Show brought us six points nearer; we now had all got a record of Puma's points and discovered none of us could add up properly. Eric thought we needed seven points; I thought we needed nine and Judy thought we needed ten. Eric was sure she would make it at Sunbury-on-Thames, at the Alsatian of the Year show, but that was a Southern show and Puma was a Northern type and rarely did well south of Leeds. That time I was right and he was wrong, as she came nowhere.

She went to Paignton and came second. No nearer, Eric wished he hadn't taken the dogs, as he broke down on the way back; breaking down with a van full of Alsatians was no joke, and he had to hire a car to bring them all home again; Sheila gave a vivid description of the journey which was one she certainly won't ever forget.

I went down to stay with my mother and my aunts, taking Janus, and going to the show at Lancing, run by the Findon Downs Dog Training Club. I had lectured to them long before I had Janus, just after I wrote *Rex* and am one of their vice-presidents. Their show is one of my favourites, as it is well organised, with all the 'stay' times worked out, so that dog 'stays' don't clash with bitch 'stays', or one class with another. The catering is superb. It is done by Doris Herman, who is married to Fred Herman, who won Cruft's in 1974 with his Collie Moss. I knew Fred long before Moss was born, when he had Sandy, his Labrador, and was thinking of buying a Collie pup, and hunting around for one. He sent me long letters describing his search and then his training, which was not easy as Moss just wouldn't learn to retrieve.

Janus did not distinguish himself, though he did do well at the little show at West Chillingham that we went to the day before. He only lost half a mark, the first time he had worked well in his life. Our improvement baffled Fred, but

I had a suspicion that it had a lot to do with the fact that there was a military band there. I sometimes train Janus to music, which he loves. He pays far more attention if we are walking to a rhythm, and I find it easier to step out to marchtime music, which brings him up close to me, walking fast. If I am slower he lags.

We had our first card for obedience; something to put beside Puma's now quite impressive line-up of red cards and red rosettes. Wilmslow were rather surprised. We were the club joke; the dog that would never make it, and the handler that couldn't handle. Very few people realised what I was up against with Janus. Those that did were all professionals. They had all come up against dogs like him. People with experience of only one or two dogs can never understand.

And the professionals had all got rid of them, not wishing to waste their time.

My time wasn't important in that sense. I didn't need show wins to prove my stock was good as I hadn't any stock to speak of; it was a hobby. So I was stuck with my dog, but determined to go on as what I learned in the ring with him would stand me in good stead one day when I got another, more carefully chosen dog. Janus can't last for ever, and it's better to plan for the future than to agonise over the inevitable.

We came home to find Puma had gained herself more points at Glasgow show, having won her novice class and come first in Junior. She now had twenty-four points. And she needed one more.

She was entered for Kirkaldy, but she came into season, seventeen weeks after her last season, much to everyone's annoyance. There was no question of me going; and Eric couldn't travel her with Judy's dogs in that condition, so she was withdrawn. She wouldn't have shown well anyway. She went to Dumfries, and was in two classes, but didn't even get placed, which wasn't very surprising as she ambled around not caring one jot about anything.

She didn't want to come out with me. She didn't want to do anything. By now she was with me, as I had decided I couldn't leave her in kennels any more; I couldn't bear to take her back and leave her; and if I wasn't going to sell her, and I wasn't, not now, with the chance of a splendid litter ahead, then I had to do something constructive and stop drifting on.

So when Kenneth and Andrew went off for a three-week cruise I decided to bring her home and get over the major hurdle in peace, without annoyance to the men. I knew there was going to be a big snag.

Kennel dogs are never house-trained, and Puma had never been inside Judy's house. Judy felt it unwise to make too much of her and attach her to them even more, as she always hoped I would take the bitch to live with me, instead of keeping her as a part-time dog.

It was obvious when I stayed with my mother that her pup was a complete success, and that I need not worry quite so much about them. If I could train Puma to be clean, my mother would happily have both dogs next year and so would my aunts, so with that hurdle surmounted, it was time to make a change in Puma's life.

Janus was now living a normal life; was great fun most of the time, though he still made me ashamed of him at shows, and neutered or not, bitches still were far more important to him than Obedience lessons. He became the club 'heat detector' and any bitch that was late was brought over to him. He soon told the owner (and everyone else) whether she was interesting or not. He was never wrong. It became a joke amongst some of us.

There were going to be problems with Puma. For one thing, she could not sleep in the house, as she was dirty at night. I cleaned out our garden shed, scrubbed it down, and put her box in there. I could clean up easily and, gradually, I hoped, she would learn the proper behaviour for a dog.

She accepted the shed philosophically, and used it as a shelter from too many people, retreating to it when family life became too much for her. She had spent hours every day shut up on her own, and she simply couldn't take the bustle of normal living that Janus now took for granted.

Mornings were wonderful, as out I went into the garden with Janus, opened Puma's door and let her out to run with him while I cleaned up the floor. I didn't know how I was going to make her realise this just wasn't done; she did respect the house most of the time during the day, except for a few accidents due usually to the fact that I was on the phone when she needed to go out. She had never needed to learn to wait.

Night was different, but if I were to take her down to my mother she had to be clean, as she would have to sleep in the house. There was nowhere outside unless I left her in the car and I didn't much fancy having to clean *that* up.

I wondered how the two dogs would work out their own relationship once Puma came home, but there was no difficulty with that. For one thing, Puma was a bitch; and Janus loves bitches, all of them, no matter what breed, from the tinest chihuahua to the biggest Great Dane. And Puma knew she was second dog, encroaching on his territory. She greeted him as she did her mother and her grandmother, legs bent, lips smiling, ears flat.

I was bothered about her night-time habits, which I knew would offend my two menfolk if they found out. They expected adult dogs to be clean all the time and found it hard to understand that she had lived a very different life to a pet dog. But I couldn't take her back.

It was great fun having two dogs. Walks are fascinating, as Janus is a ground scenter, telling me about rabbit and hare and fox and stoat; Puma air scents, her head held high, and the wrinkling of her nostrils is followed by her eager eyes. I see a squirrel chasing through the trees, a hundred yards or more beyond us. Her ears are so alert she hears a rabbit running a hundred feet away; or a cat crossing the road. She runs to look, alerting both me and Janus, whose nose is more sensitive, but whose hearing isn't nearly so acute, possibly because of those long flap ears.

Puma guarded from the start. She had always guarded me, regarding me as her person when we were at shows together, ready to bark at people who startled me, as I discovered one day in some canteen, sitting opposite Judy.

A breeder Judy knew came across the room, unseen by me. Puma was under the table. Without thinking, he put his hand on my shoulder and leaned across me to talk to Judy. I hadn't seen him come, and jumped. Puma exploded.

'I'm an idiot,' he said. 'I breed Alsatians and I know them, and I knew Puma was there. She's a very good guard dog.'

I was glad it was an Alsatianist; other people don't always understand and attribute ferocity to the breed, when in fact they only bark to alert people. Of course, there are rogues, but in one year, of nearly nine hundred dogs in the country that bit people badly enough for them to have hospital treatment, only five were Alsatians.

Reports exaggerate. There were two escaped human criminal killers last week; but that doesn't make all men dangerous.

Much of the worry over health hazards from dogs is equally exaggerated, as a recent report by a public health lecturer stated that diseases from dogs come 793rd on the list of human hazards. Decently kept dogs are no risk at all. It is the strays and those in families where hygiene rates low that cause trouble. I have never caught anything from my animals, but other humans infect me with colds or gastric flu at least once every year, and I didn't get mumps from my cat; I caught it from my son.

The pity of it is that often when scare reports come out, vets are brought healthy animals to put down because parents have become frightened. The children suffer far more from losing a favourite pet than they do from the possible risk of catching something from it.

Chapter 9

Very few people, even dog owners, realise what it is like to try and resettle an older dog. Puma had led a totally different life with Judy. She had spent her days outside, in an unheated barn, summer and winter alike. She found the house too hot.

She had spent a great deal of her time behind bars. The door of her private pen, which was about eight feet long and four feet wide, with a bench at the back, and a concrete floor, was barred, so that the dog could see out.

She only felt safe behind bars in the house.

This proved very difficult, as the only bars there were, were on our dining room chairs, so that I made Puma her own little pen, where she could curl up and feel safe, and look at the world, as she had for eighteen months, from between wooden slats. It kept the world away from her. She didn't like people coming too close and she couldn't get used to them rushing into the room where she was lying quietly, not only behind the chairs, but also behind me. I was the only familiar person now in her new world; she had lost Judy and Marian and Sheila; she had lost her kennel mates and her runs in the field; and she had a whole load of new rules to learn.

Previously she emptied when she felt like it, on the ground of her pen.

That was no longer acceptable and it worried her, as possibly she felt she shouldn't do it at all, anywhere, and she became extremely anxious after a few days, running round the garden until she burst. I praised her, as it was in the right place, and she relaxed a little; next time was easier, but it took several days to reassure her about that.

I didn't want her anxious. We still needed that last point for her Junior Warrant. Time was passing and it would be maddening to miss it by only one point. There were no big shows for some time, and the next championship show would be too late. She'd be more than eighteen months old—no longer eligible.

She had so much to learn. She ate her food like a wild animal, savaging it, and the plate. I couldn't help her know me by feeding her from my hands; she would have had my fingers off, as she was so hungry for food, which was probably her main reassurance, the only familiar thing in her life. She snapped when I offered her a biscuit. So I did the next best thing and mixed all her food with my hands, to try and get her to associate my smell with eating, and with comfort.

I couldn't feed her anywhere near Janus as she tried to eat his food too.

The cats couldn't stand her. She chased them mercilessly, often trapping one of them under a bed, baying, as she tried to get at it, not to harm, but to lick. Casey slashed at her, and Chia fled, on to the highest piece of furniture she could find, and yelled at the top of her voice. Casey never yelled at Puma; he used his claws and I didn't want her eyes scratched.

Janus watched in surprise. He wasn't allowed to chase cats, and it dawned on him that Puma wasn't either, so when she did, he barked to tell me she was at it again. She had been able to chase cats all she liked at Judy's, where the cats could run and jump on to wall or barn. There were at least seven cats; possibly more, and no one had time to stop the dogs running after them. No cat was ever harmed. Though some of the dogs did get scratched and learned that way that it was better to leave Puss alone. One of Judy's moggies is immense and a doughty fighter. The dogs avoid him!

We went to a show at Crewe, run by Liverpool Alsatian Club. It was an open. If we could gain that last one point, we would have that warrant.

It was mid August and the entry was small, most people being away on holiday. There were only three bitches in Puma's class and she won it easily. It didn't feel to me like a point at all, as I would rather come up against real competition in a big class, but we had the warrant and a few weeks later at 16½ months in a much bigger class she came first again and I felt we had won our way there. It was a tremendous achievement; Judy had been breeding all her life, but even so there weren't many of her dogs with a warrant to their name. It was a bigger achievement for her than for me; for me it was a bonus, for her it was a professional triumph.

I determined to use that winter, when there is very little doing in the show world, to get Puma house-trained, and used to household noises; a dog in kennels hears outside noises only. Janus took the ticking clock for granted. He knew about radio and television and the bang made by the washing machine as it changed programmes. I hadn't thought about such things for over three years. I had to start thinking in puppy terms all over again with Puma, and one tends not to, with an adult dog, forgetting lack of experience. If we were alone she emerged, to lie close against me, her muzzle on my shoe, while I tried to remember Janus's early days. This was a dog that had never seen a wide variety of places; never had to contend with household noises; she was used only to the sound of the trees; to barks and to other dogs, and to traffic.

The first time I drew the curtains she bolted upstairs

under a bed and I had to coax her out. The first time I switched on my transistor radio she barked at it, her ruff raised, her ears alert; the first time she saw television she rushed at it, barking angrily.

The washing machine flipped her; the vacuum cleaner sent her upstairs again; or she would run to the back door, eyes agonised, begging to be shut away in that outhouse again, on her own, away from so much stimulation. I put her there whenever she asked, but not for too long.

She had to learn to live with us; she had to learn to accept house noises; she had to learn to be clean indoors. She had had no more training than the six-week pup straight from kennels; and she was as unknowing as a child who is brought up in a plastic bubble.

Walks were fine; the park was fine, but home, we reverted to agony again. I put her on her lead, in the house, the loop through my belt, and worked with her attached to me, so that if she baulked, I knew at once and could kneel down and comfort her.

Slowly she learned to accept the noises in the house. Slowly she learned not to make messes indoors; she always chose the spare-room, presumably because it wasn't used, and wasn't part of our territory. Luckily Janus is exceptionally clean and never once cocked a leg after she had puddled. He merely looked at me as if to say, 'I don't do that, do I?'

One day when I was sure she was safe to keep in the house, I found a mess in the hall. I wasn't sure which dog was responsible as Puma had been good for several weeks, so took both to it, said 'BAD' in a very fierce voice and cleaned up.

Janus asked to go out.

We went out, and there in the middle of the lawn where he never went, he produced his own effort which proved it couldn't possibly have been him who misbehaved in the hall. I praised him, and he tore round the garden,

137

greyhounding, delighted to have shown me he was a good dog.

It was the last time Puma ever did mess the house. Now she asks to go out. Even if she is feeling very sick she manages to hang on till we get outside, which is something even Janus can't do.

The panicky rushing from kitchen to dining-room continued for over a month, noticeably at its worst when other people were there. With me, she was at ease, coming to be cuddled, putting her paws over my legs, her face anxious. Am I doing the right thing? What *is* it you want of me? Is this the right place to be? She was always very worried.

Back at Judy's she relaxed, ran again in the field, becoming exceedingly excited as soon as she saw the field where the horses and cattle grazed; racing flat out, delighted with herself, a different dog.

'You can't keep her, Joyce. She'll never settle,' my vet said one day. He had come to lunch and Puma had flipped again. I was feeling the same way; she didn't really relate to me; she didn't seem to relate to anyone; and I wished with all my heart that either I had never bought her or that I had had the guts to sell her back to Judy. But though she didn't seem attached to me, I was attached to her, and I hate accepting defeat.

She would have nothing whatever to do with Kenneth or Andrew, which didn't help in the least. She had never been looked after by men; and she was suspicious of them. With both my dogs I seemed to have bought a load of problems.

She and Janus adored one another. Janus had another dog to play with; they ran in the garden, engaging in mock battles, biting in play at one another's cheeks; wrestling and romping. In the garden, out of doors, Puma was a different animal. She never played with me; she hadn't a clue how to play with people, but with Janus she had a riot.

We were just starting to get somewhere when she had

her third season. Puma's seasons were something on their own; she was sick in the mornings and had a very upset tummy for most of the time. She flirted outrageously with Janus, and I drove miles to walk her right away from other dogs (Janus being neutered was no problem) and to avoid callers at the door.

The season ended and she began to gain weight. Not a little weight, but a lot of weight. She began to guard herself, and to warn Janus off. I took her to the vet. Surely some dog couldn't have got at her?

He examined her. It was a phantom pregnancy. It was only now we realised what had been wrong before. She continued to think she was pregnant for the full nine weeks after the day she would have been mated. She was lethargic and ravenous; and very thirsty. She wouldn't play with Janus, but lay and panted until I was sure the vet had been wrong.

She dug holes under the veronica bush. Large holes, into which she dropped and lay with her nose out saying, 'Don't come near me. This is where I'm having the pups.' One day she stole a jersey and carefully lined the muddy hole with that.

Then she developed milk. And that night, at about three in the morning she squealed. I went down. She was pacing up and down the outhouse floor, stopping to strain and squeal again, saying, 'I'm having pups and you're not helping.'

The vet had said if she did that to be very firm and take her for a walk to distract her as he guaranteed there was nothing there. There was a lot of milk, and she seemed to be in pain, and I could hardly take her for a walk at that time of night.

I dressed, and got a book to read so that I could sit by her and keep her from disturbing the two men. 'Help,' she'd squeal and I'd say sharply: 'Don't be stupid. Get down,' knowing how dogs act to the gallery. Sympathise and they are so sorry for themselves you think they'll die next minute. Some people are like that too. Sympathy isn't always a good idea.

By morning Puma had settled down and decided OK there weren't any pups after all. Instead she decided the cats were her pups. She and Casey by now had an armed truce. She learned not to bay out loud. Instead she did it under her breath, a funny wailing bawl that sent me looking upstairs to find a cat, demented, penned under a bed swiping at her face with his claws, while she roared with laughter.

Aren't I funny?

Puma loves being funny, but only for me.

Not funny. I sorted out dog and rescued cat. Now after her nine weeks of imagination she didn't want to chase them for the hell of it; she decided they were puppies, and every time she came up to one, she put a paw on it and gave it a swift and thorough bath. The cats loathed it. Other cats suffer too. I was told of one bitch who also had phantom pregnancies and insisted on dragging the family cat, an immense tom, much older and larger than she was, by the scruff of his neck, into her basket. Surprisingly, he endured it stoically. Casey never endures anything stoically. If he doesn't want to be touched, he bites, animal and human alike.

Janus had to endure her attentions too. He was puzzled by her intensity and her lack of all desire to play. She only wanted to get her paw on him and clean him up too. He would stand there, looking extremely sheepish, but he wouldn't allow her to cuddle him close. With an offended air he got up and removed himself as far from her as possible.

It soon became very plain it was pointless showing Puma for at least two weeks before a season was due as she was lethargic, and became intensely anxious about everything; it was pointless showing her for nine weeks after, as she

140

bloated, and went around looking very broody and acting broodier than any bitch I'd seen.

And it soon became apparent that seasons for Puma were not twice a year; they were dead on time every seventeen weeks, and a major nuisance, except that she kept herself most beautifully clean.

Bert, Judy's partner's husband, gave me one very useful tip when we met at a show.

'If she starts getting broody, cut her rations; in the last week, ration her water; just a few sips every hour. She won't bloat and she won't come into milk.'

It worked. Though she was still likely to inform me she was sure she was having puppies, even if the vet did say no, and suppose I came and helped.

What with two weeks off before seasons, three weeks with seasons and a nine-week broodiness, she was off song for fourteen weeks in every sixteen. The remaining two she was extremely alert and lively and very mischievous; but between her and Janus I began to wonder if I was ever going to have a reasonable spell with my two dogs. It was pointless even trying obedience with Puma—she was never able to concentrate on anything but her own feelings.

Janus meanwhile was beginning to sober down a little; to have some idea of what Obedience was about. So long as I watched his diet rigidly and always remembered his trypsin additive, and watched his exercise, he stayed well, and we were able to go to the club regularly. I was still going to Wilmslow. I wanted to start Puma more seriously as she needed discipline but Judy and Eric were afraid I would ruin her for shows, and as I hadn't paid anything like her full price and Judy was to have two pups back as part payment, I didn't feel she was totally mine; so I only took her occasionally to work, mainly in stays, and never taught her to 'sit' when we halted, as normal dogs do; she stood when I halted. I had no intention anyway of doing competition Obedience with her. She was my brood bitch.

141

The culmination of a long-standing ambition nursed for almost all my life.

Slowly she was beginning to fit into the household. She wanted nothing to do with anyone but me, and even with me she was not very responsive in many ways. If we went out, Janus nearly burst with pleasure when we returned, bringing his toys to us, tail going madly, body weaving, groaning with delight. Puma met us quietly, no effusion in her. I didn't know if it was her odd hormone balance, as by now the vet felt she had too much of her female hormones to be good for her; or bringing her home late; or just that she was a less responsive animal; or perhaps it was the result of lead poisoning as that in children can cause brain damage.

She never wanted to play with me. If I threw a ball she stood and looked at me. 'You potty or something?' Whereas Janus accelerated into speedtrack racing to get it, and bring it back and chuck it at me to throw back at him.

All in all, I wasn't very happy about her. This time I only had to say to Judy, 'Puma isn't settling. Will you buy her back?' and she'd have leaped at the chance, as when we did have good days in shows, she won. We had to pick our days; a total waste of money to take her anywhere within those critical weeks.

That summer I went down to stay with my mother, with both dogs. I wanted to go to the Findon Downs show again and as you can't take spare dogs to a show the only thing to do was to enter Puma for competition too. I could always scratch when I got there. I knew a bit more about Janus now. I had been trying to work him as if he were a Collie; and he is a gundog. We needed a very different approach. Collies can take a working attitude and lap it up; they are bred that way.

All the gundogs are extremely boisterous, very playful, and mature late. Turn work into a game with Janus and I got instant co-operation. Try and be more sober and I lost out, with a sulking dog indulging in dumb insolence. He would do it at the slowest pace I have ever seen; absolutely accurate and moving like a snail.

I learned that with him I had to restrict praise or he rioted; I had to play-train or he rebelled; and if there were bitches anywhere near season, or the smell of food, I might as well not bother, as he gets distracted and you can't correct a dog in the ring. It's against the rules. And what he gets away with on one occasion he will get away with on a second, and by then he makes a habit of it.

We went down to my mother's, both dogs travelling in the back of my Mini. We stopped for long walks and made a holiday of the journey as it's nearly 300 miles, and is easier taken that way.

We arrived and greeted my mother, and I took the dogs in. Lucky, her Westie, wasn't too sure about these immense animals, and retreated behind her chair, her small face poking out, watching. Janus vanished and reappeared a moment later with the toy seal that stands on my mother's bedside table. He had remembered for a whole year! We removed it, and took the dogs out to run in the garden. Lucky tagged after them, soon shouting 'wait for me', and from then on all was well.

The day of the show was very hot. I worked Janus, not well but passably and then commented to the Beginner judge that I intended to scratch Puma as she was Breed trained, had had very little Obedience training and wasn't ready to show; I had really only entered her so that I could bring her into the grounds.

'You paid, and I don't mind,' the judge said. 'I won't put your score down, but she has to learn the difference between Breed and Obedience sometime, so try her.'

I had tried her once before, when she gaited in front of me all the way at a fast pace, and stood at the halt, instead of walking at heel and sitting when I stopped, bolted to the car when let off lead in the ring, and generally panicked.

143

But I had paid, and the judge didn't mind, so I decided to work Puma. Janus had lost only one mark, for two minor faults at a ½ each, so she did know I could work a dog. We had gained 99%.

Puma decided to panic; she didn't like people behind her and kept turning to look at them, as if she were haunted; she did gait and she did stand, and then when I said 'sit' more sharply she half lowered herself, thought 'O Heavens no' and half stood, in the oddest attitude, looking agitated. She did a lovely recall, couldn't get to me fast enough from all that way across the ring, and then walked out, and looked at her dumbbell as if she had never seen one before in her life.

All in all it was pretty ghastly.

The judge gave me some helpful advice, including trying to get her into a ring more often to accustom her to being there on her own instead of with about twenty other Alsatians, as she is in the Breed ring. It was rather like making a beauty queen take up Olympic gymnastics.

'I won't do Novice with her,' I said.

That is the next class up. If you win the Beginner class twice you can never enter it again, even with a brand new pup. You start in Novice.

'I would. Just tell the judge what you told me, and ask her not to put the marks on the score sheet. She won't mind.' The judge was considerate, helpful and kind.

Novice that day was for bitches or dogs. Beginner had not divided them. I worked Janus in the dog novice ring, and came about tenth, which at that stage pleased me as we were coming up from the bottom, it was a very big class, and we were up against experienced handlers there.

I told the Novice bitch judge Puma had been in about a hundred Breed rings, and this was our first Obedience show of any size and she was very *in*experienced. The judge looked at me, and said nothing. I asked her not to put our score down as we weren't really competing, but I had a feeling she wasn't listening to me.

Puma decided to act the fool, and I became more and more nervous with her. She decided she was scared stiff of the posts on the corners; and she didn't like the dogs round the ring so she shied off them; she behaved abominably, and on her recall, instead of sitting in front of me and waiting to be told to go round my back and sit at heel, she went straight to heel. Dumbbell? I just had to be joking.

We finished.

The judge came across and proceeded to give me a long lecture which did nothing whatever to help my confidence; in fact it was a very effective and destructive lecture which ensured that I made a mess of Puma for weeks afterwards. It was an undeserved lecture, as she told me I was too cocky and thought I could do Obedience when I couldn't.

Bewildered, I put Puma in the car with Janus and went for lunch.

The judge was sitting opposite me and suddenly said to her steward who was sitting beside me, 'Did you hear that woman who said she had been in Breed with the bitch and was now trying Obedience as they were very experienced? I put her in her place.'

Oh boy, she did. I hadn't gone in with much confidence, and she had done such a good job of destroying the little bit I had, through not listening properly, Puma and I were set back weeks, as my worries about her began to show when we worked at the dog club or anywhere else. I even began to slip back with Janus, as the lecture had had a soul-destroying effect, and I decided I just wasn't cut out for Obedience at all and might as well give up.

But I am an obstinate cuss, and I suddenly thought: 'I'll show them. Somehow.'

I didn't know how. But I would find out how to get the best of my two dogs and do it, and I would get Puma socialised if it killed me; she still didn't care much for

145

people in mass. Or even some that visited us, though she no longer ran in that insane crouch from one room to another as if something were about to leap on her and eat her.

I took her to shows with Janus. I entered her, not to do well, but to try and get her used to rings on her own, used to walking at heel and not belting full out; and used to facing all the incidents that can happen at shows. And decided we were there for the benefit of learning how to work together. To hell with prizes.

But of course we were foiled by those wretched seasons; for about twelve weeks out of every sixteen it was as much use trying to train her as it would be to try and dye the sea pink. She was the laziest bitch I have ever seen. She did excel at long downstays. She'd do those for ever.

Away from the shows and the club, life was far easier. The dogs loved their walks in the park. Out every day, sit them on stay by my car while I locked it and got out gloves and leads and a quoit to throw, and then a pat on the head and the words 'Good dog'. And off they went.

And a year later, after racking my brains as to why my dogs always riot when I say 'Good dog,' the penny dropped. When I say 'Good dog,' it doesn't mean that at all. It means: 'OK. Off you go now. Stay's ended. Have a ball.' But I didn't realise it till I inadvertently said it at the club one night and both my dogs went crazy, racing round the hall making themselves most unpopular. My club praise is 'Clever lad' or 'Clever girl'; Good dog means something else. I hadn't realised how one can have a disobedient dog through one's own lack of thought, till then. Now I watch my words as well as my gestures, as you can fool the dog with those. Say, 'Don't drop it'—and the only word the dog recognises is drop—and he does. Not his fault—it's ours, for not realising how simple his mind is.

Chapter 10

That year we had a rare treat. Kenneth had a few days of holiday over after boating. He suggested we go to Scotland for a long weekend; we could take Janus, but Puma, who was still not clean at night and still slept in the outhouse, would be a problem. Judy offered to have her back for those few days. She settled in at once, going to her old kennel and jumping on to the bench as if she had never left it.

Janus fretted all the way home. By morning, when it was plain we were to go off in the car, he seemed to have forgotten. Whenever the dogs are coming, I pack their things first; leads, bowls, food. That way, they know they are coming, and there is no fretting. If you leave their stuff to last, they don't know, and become miserable.

Janus brought his own contribution. I had forgotten his blanket. I found it lying in a muddled heap on the garage floor beside the car and his stock of food, and his trypsin capsules. Those are always my first requirement. I keep a spare tin in my handbag and another in my car, as it's useless trying to feed him without.

We have tried, several times, to see if he can digest; but he tips the food back undigested during the night. And I didn't want that in a hotel bedroom.

We were lucky with the weather; off at dawn, into a day

stolen from time; the trees brilliant with autumn, berried red, leaves coloured, each new vista even better than the last as we sped along the motorway leaving the towns behind us. Once we had staggered that way in an old car with three carsick children and stopped near Beattock summit for the night; now we were at Beattock within four hours of leaving Manchester. It was unbelievable.

It was also difficult to believe we had actually got away without one of the firm's ever recurrent crises to send Kenneth round the world and back. The hotel was comfortable; the food was excellent; our bedroom, slightly Victorian and somewhat Spartan, was clean and the bed was good; we had our own bathroom and Janus slept by our bed.

We arrived at tea time; a real Scottish meal with bread and butter and jam, scones and cakes, and a good dark tea, served in the lounge, where an elderly Labrador sat with hungry eyes watching us. I don't like dogs fed at table and he went unrewarded as he was much too plump. Janus was upstairs as the lounge belonged to the Lab.

There was a parrot in a cage on a table by the stairs. He was an amusing bird with a varied vocabulary, and we stopped to admire him and chat with him. I thought very little more about him until, going upstairs with Janus, the dog suddenly scented the bird.

He put his head through the bannisters to see what was below. The cage was within touching distance of his nose. I had never imagined a parrot could have a nervous breakdown, but this one did.

There was an immense stinking dog's head within inches of his nose. The poor bird dropped to the floor of his cage, lying on his back and screamed, an eldritch yell that startled everybody and brought the landlord running while I tried to yank Janus back through the bannisters, which wasn't all that easy as he was totally fascinated.

Poor parrot was removed and spent most of the rest of

our visit on his owner's shoulder, looking nervously around to see if the dog was there.

We walked. We walked through the forests, looking out to the Kyles of Bute, to the massed trees, ablaze with autumn colour. We walked along little lanes, and on sandy beaches, watching the silken sea slip slowly up the shore, hearing the seethe and murmur and whisper of the caressing waves. The sun shone for us.

We drove, out along the coast roads, looking at breathtaking views; pulling up as an ancient stag, one antlered, seedy, and disreputable with his lopsided head, stood in the middle of the road, calmly looking at us. The car windows were all closed; there was no scent to warn him of dangerous humans. His coat was grey with age. He should have been up on the hills, roaring his rage at the other rutting stags, while his harem grazed peacefully, but he was plainly now a loner, a has-been, an outcast. His mild eyes watched, and then he crossed to the wire fence and, no longer able to vault it, wriggled himself between two strands and cantered over the moor.

A mile further on we drew into the roadside again to watch a Peregrine Falcon serene on his watching post, as he surveyed the land, looking for food.

Civilisation was very far away.

On our last night we walked at the edge of the beach, and something alerted Janus. He was away, and I realised there were sheep loose on the shingle. I had already had one warning with Janus when we parked near the slaughterhouse and he was so excited I knew I would have trouble. Luckily the beach was very uneven and I caught him and leashed him and that was the end of his free running. He has no intention of obeying if something catches his attention that attracts him more than I do; and now I know him, I don't run risks. I have learned to try and prevent trouble, not court it.

It was time to go home, back along the motorway, to run

149

into dense fog near Warrington and spend an unnerving hour. Back to fetch Puma, who didn't seem overjoyed to see us. Pleased, but not excited. She came home, and life went on again.

It a was slightly easier life as I had given up both lectures and the chairmanship of the Children's Book Group when my father was ill, and I decided not to start either again. I was very busy with writing; and I wanted time for my dogs. I wanted more time to get out and about, too, as a writer doesn't get new material by sitting at home doing nothing. You need constant recharging; new places; new ideas. Often first impressions are more vivid than any afterwards; familiarity makes it difficult to see objectively, so the more I went about and the more I saw, the more I had to write about, and the better it was for the dogs.

I was still going to dog club on Wednesdays. Puma didn't seem to progress; she was edgy, often looking behind her, and nothing I did with her seemed to work. She needed a great deal of reassurance all the time.

Just after Christmas, when she was at the vet for recurrent ear trouble, I mentioned that the false pregnancies were still happening.

'I think she'd better be mated next season,' he said. 'She's destined for pups, and she'll be nearly two. It might settle her as well.'

Judy agreed, and we began to look for a stud dog in real earnest. We looked at one after the other at the shows. Puma has a pale muzzle, and many judges prefer dark muzzles; so we wanted a very dark dog. And we wanted one with a really gorgeous disposition. We looked at dogs at shows; some weren't dark enough for Puma; some would be too similar in breeding to her and we didn't want close breeding.

We narrowed it to two dogs. One in Hastings, and Champion Rossfort Premonition near at home; in Yorkshire. She was due to come into season in March. I watched her like a hawk, swabbing her as the time came near so that we could get the day just right. A bitch is only fertile for three out of the twenty-one days. Get it wrong and you waste time and the stud fee, and have a barren bitch as well.

We still weren't sure whether to go to Hastings. We could stay with my mother. No problem there. Judy wanted to come too as a maiden bitch is not always easy to mate and she could ensure nothing went wrong. We would use Premonition on Puma next time; a year and a half later.

Then came the fuel crisis, and threats of petrol rationing. No petrol to be had locally, and everything very difficult. Hastings was out of the question. We only got petrol at home because we were regular customers; my Mini only held five gallons at a time and we might well be marooned.

So we would go to Premonition this time and to the dog in Hastings next. The bitch goes to the dog; otherwise the poor stud dog would be for ever on the move and his owner would never get anything done. Mrs Hunter very kindly offered to meet us halfway, to save our petrol, as we might well not be able to get any casually anywhere.

Meanwhile it wasn't yet March and Puma was to go to Olympia, to Cruft's, for which she had qualified. She was able to go, as her season was later. It would be, when the dog was booked.

By now I was part-time relief teacher at Parr's Wood, the Friday Manchester Education Authority evening class on dog management and training. Marian, who had helped Judy when Puma was small, was Head Trainer, and had asked if I would like to help, as she was never able to have an evening off, and I had already stepped in one evening when she had flu and no one else was able to teach.

Marian offered to drive us down. We asked Brian if he would take the dog class for us and set off. I drove to Wilmslow, to put my Mini in Marian's garage, and we started at midnight. It was February and very cold. Puma seemed to think we were mad. She would have much preferred to go to bed. She settled by my feet, where the heater warmed her.

We stopped in a service station to exercise her.

Up and down, by torchlight in the freezing cold, and the dark, among the parked lorries, their drivers snoozing, among the many cars that came and went, among the many dogs that appeared suddenly from all over the country; all breeds, all converging on that one place for that coveted award, Best in Show at Cruft's; or to win the Obedience championship; best dog or best bitch in the country.

Puma was obliging. She walked. But do anything? Not she. Here? You don't mean it, oh come on do, let's go back to the car and go to sleep.

We had blankets and pillows, as well as coffee and food. At Watford Gap after another abortive walk we rolled up in our blankets. It was two in the morning and bitterly cold, with flurries of snow. We agreed we were mad.

Marian slept at the back; I was in front; getting colder and colder. I finally woke, stiff and freezing, to find Puma had cleverly snitched my blanket, wound herself neatly up in it, in a cocoon and was warm and very snug. I tried to pour coffee silently, but Marian woke up. She had been wrapped in her rug, but was also cold and stiff. We looked at our watches. Just after four. We took ourselves to the cloakroom, tried Puma again without avail and decided to push on.

It was as well we did, because Marian hadn't driven in London before and we hadn't realised the London rush hour began so early. We became part of a milling mass of maniac motorists and I was reduced to prayer. Marian gritted her teeth and drove on. We had an AA route map with us, but the instructions for reaching the North Circular road were ambiguous and we didn't reach it.

152

We tried to ask the way but Londoners at that time in the morning don't even reply. I asked fourteen people. The fifteenth did stop.

'Ee, luv, yer right out of yer way.' It was a delightful broad North country accent; he gave us copious directions, asked us to give his love to Burnley and vanished, unaware that he had made our day and made us feel people weren't so bad, after all. So long as they were Northerners, though Marian's people live in Harrow, and I was born in Kent.

We got lost again.

This time Puma was obviously so cramped that I took her with me, into a police station, where she put her paws on the desk and interrogated the sergeant, who grinned and said, 'Three guesses. You want Olympia.'

I agreed.

Only he had no idea how to direct us; it would be too confusing, but he could direct us to Wormwood Scrubbs. He went there every day! We reached Wormwood Scrubbs, but didn't know who to ask and then Marian pulled in at the lights beside a taxi driver.

'Olympia?' she yelled.

'Follow me,' he yelled back.

We did. By the time we reached Olympia we both needed brandy.

Olympia is daunting. We went inside. The Alsatians were miles from anywhere; Puma's number was way up in the 3,000s; we found everything up to 2,500 and then there was a gap, but at last we got sorted out, put her on her bench and went to have breakfast.

Breakfast over, we went to find Puma.

We'd lost her.

We asked an attendant. The numbers didn't go up to 3,000, he said.

I remembered the horrible story of the girl who came to London with her mother, and went off shopping. When she went back to her hotel everyone denied having seen either of them; and the room was different. The mother had developed cholera while the daughter was out and they tried to cover up. I had visions of Puma lost, or stolen, or off her bench with the chain broken and began to feel panicky.

We found her again, after a search that lasted nearly thirty-five minutes. It was time to exercise her. She loathed the exercise area. It disgusted her (me too) and no, she wasn't going. Not at all. Not ever.

I couldn't find her bench again but I ran into Judy who was there with some of her own dogs, and we went together to the benches. Later when I wanted to visit the Ladies, I took Puma too. This time we got lost together. I could find Chows and Dalmatians and Rottweilers and Setters, but find the German Shepherds, no.

I was meeting my agent, and presently Pat did find us, and we went together round the dogs. Another friend who was due to meet me arrived but never found me at all. Olympia is like that.

By lunchtime I made the horrible discovery that I felt exceedingly sick and very shivery, and my head ached abominably. Pat had gone, and Marian was with Judy and her dogs. I curled up beside Puma, not wanting to move, wishing I was in bed, warm and safe, not here, in this ghastly hall with everybody in the world walking past us staring at us. 'Is she for sale?' 'No.' I began to be afraid she might be stolen, and I don't like benched dogs anyway. One of our Northern members had his dog stolen off a bench at Liverpool last year; Jerry never found the dog again. It does happen. I only had a feeling then, but if I have to bench my dog, I try never to leave her there alone.

Apart from anything else someone might feed her something or harm her; there are peculiar people about.

Puma's class came up at one o'clock. Eric was there, beautifully dressed in newly pressed silver grey flannels and a navy blue blazer. I handed Puma to him, and he put on

154

her special collar and lead. Round the ring she went, with over thirty other bitches. Stood to be looked at which she did beautifully. And then I realised she was terrified of the noise and the vast spaces and of the crowds. Her ears showed she was very tense indeed.

Eric led her up to the judge to be examined. The judge opened Puma's mouth and panic did the rest. She emptied herself completely in the ring, just missing Eric's shoes, the most heinous crime that any dog can commit. Eric glared at me. I heard somebody say, 'Why on earth didn't they exercise that bitch?' I thought of the freezing cold hours pacing round and round every blasted motorway service station between Manchester and London; the long walk at the end; the hour spent in the exercise area. Poor Puma had clammed up completely in horror and there's nothing any owner can do about that.

She came eighth which was respectable in that competition at that class. Eric handed her back to me. He'd had to clean up the ring.

'Take your bloody bitch. Why didn't you exercise her?'

'I did; for hours and hours and hours!'

I don't think he believed me. We crawled on to her bench together, and I sat feeling more and more wretchedly ill. Judy and Jess came up to talk and then Judy brought Mrs Hunter over to see Puma and I managed to drag myself up and go and look at Premonition. He was gorgeous and we booked him then and there, as everything about him was perfect for Puma. He hadn't been in his class yet. That was still to come.

We were allowed to leave early because of heating restrictions. We had a long way to go, and Premonition still hadn't been shown when we left. It wasn't till next day I discovered he had been Best of Breed that day. The journey home was horrible; broken briefly near Harrow by schoolboys doing a census.

'Where had we been?'

'To a dog show,' I said wearily.

'Well, that's different, anyway,' the bright voice assured me. Most other people had been to the office. It was a Friday.

We reached Marian's house again about midnight. I got out of my car and drove home, feeling very dodgy indeed. I took it slowly, not sure if I would survive. Puma, relieved to find herself somewhere familiar, was soundly asleep. I got home and let her into the garden.

'Thank heaven,' she said. At last she could relax and empty herself in comfort. She can still be an absolute pest in that respect if we are away for a whole day. Except that it is an advantage if I bring her to London—she's absolutely safe—she can't go!

I crawled into bed. By morning I had a raging temperature and flu and felt very sorry for myself. And we discovered that Puma wouldn't go into the garden at all unless I was there; and she wouldn't eat her food unless I was there. So her food came up by my bed, and I put on all the clothes I had and staggered down to the French windows when she needed to go out, cursing her dismally.

Somehow I don't think I am of the right stuff for Cruft's. I like the little shows best; the laughter and the relaxation; not a vast mob of strangers, all so intent on their own affairs that the rest of the world doesn't exist for them.

Chapter 11

Unfortunately, although the books say bitches have regular seasons, dogs don't read. Puma, up to Cruft's, had been dead on seventeen weeks. We had worked out the next date, and warned Mrs Hunter when she was likely to be due. No sensible stud dog owner uses him too frequently and we didn't want to find he had mated a bitch the day before Puma and wasn't available. Even if we'd tried, he might not have made it. No dog is inexhaustible and, over-used, even sex becomes a bore to him.

So of course this time Puma didn't stick to her usual cycle. The eighteenth week started, and I rang Judy.

'Not a trace.'

'I hope she hasn't decided to go back to a normal six months, now we've booked the dog,' Judy said.

The nineteenth week began.

Bingo. The swab was positive and there we were, this time even more anxious to watch she didn't escape and that no intruder got in. We rang Mrs Hunter. Judy told me to watch for maximum swelling, and the loss of colour in the discharge. I didn't really need to bother as by the twelfth day Puma was inviting Janus, and even on occasion offering herself to Casey who was rather bewildered by this odd flirtation.

'Right,' Judy said. 'She's ready.'

We were to meet the dog in a field close to the trans-Pennine motorway, midway for both of us. Petrol was still a problem but I had an account at my garage, and was a regular customer so was allowed my ration without needing to beg. Marian was coming with us too.

The mating of a valuable bitch to a valuable dog is a major affair. A maiden bitch may prove so wild that the dog can't get near her, or she may attack him, not having experienced this sort of thing before. She may get bored and try to lie down, ruining the dog for ever. Some bitches aren't all sex-minded.

Mating of dogs is peculiar in every way, as the dog mounts the bitch, and once inside her, he swells to huge proportions and is held, locked, by a muscle in the vagina, so tying. Until the swelling collapses any movement on the part of the bitch will result in major injury.

So breeders ensure that several people are there, to hold the animals steady as the tie may last for three-quarters of an hour. Furthermore, though the dog starts in a mounted position, nature has enabled him to turn himself so both are tail to tail, back to back. No one quite knows why. It has been thought that in the wild state such a long mating makes them vulnerable to attack and both have their heads free to bite; but I can't imagine two mating animals indulging in a fight.

Many people think the change in position is wrong and one vet even wrote that the dog should be forcibly tied so that he can't turn round; a statement that caused a great deal of hilarity among breeders used to the procedure.

Puma might be difficult; she might be too tight to mate, and perhaps need stretching. We had to make sure she hadn't had a meal for twenty-four hours. Once at Judy's kennels, Sheila forgot the stud dog was to mate and the bitch's owners were too soft-hearted to leave their bitch without food. They had a wasted journey as the two

158

animals curled up, nestled against one another and slept off their meals, not in the least interested in sex.

Janus of course had to be left at home. He was taking second place at this time, as all his problems seemed to be solved. He had now reached the normal weight for a Golden Retriever dog; so long as I didn't get him soaked he wasn't rheumaticky; and so long as I never walked him more than three miles at a stretch, that leg remained sound. He still walks as if he had a broken back, but it doesn't bother him. He has changed in temperament too now he is fit; he had been a lugubrious dog, sometimes a very mournful dog. Now he is a joyous nut.

He adored Puma, but kept her in her place. He took both bones; he had the best bed; he took every toy away from her. He was unquestionably cock dog and also rather dog in the manger, apt to collect all the dogs' belongings, put them in his corner and lie there on guard, daring her to come near.

She had her own cure for that.

One day she wanted the bone, but Janus had both. She ran to the window and barked. I looked out.

Nothing there.

Janus went to look and Puma flew across the room, seized the bone and tucked herself behind a chair in an ungetatable corner. After a few minutes Janus realised he'd been had and went to her, but this time she prevailed.

Next time he wasn't caught. He looked up at her and went on gnawing.

She raced into the hall and bellowed at the front door. Millions of men here. As Janus roared out, she raced in, once more got the bone and took it off. She could hold her own, but she did it the cunning way. Between the two methods, she often did manage to get it off him. If I took it and gave it to her he grabbed it back as soon as I forgot to watch him.

They never fought. Mock battles and hilarious romps,

159

which had to be curtailed now she was in season as, though Janus was neutered, the old instincts were there, and pretty strong. The flirtations were checked, and both dogs put on down stays, which were so difficult for them that by the end of five minutes they were exhausted by the effort to keep still when they wanted to play, and they went to sleep.

Janus watched us leave the house, paws on the window sill, ears back, eyes forlorn. A long howl followed us.

It was a bitterly cold March day.

We found the roundabout leading to the field without difficulty. The field was fenced all round with chain link wires, eight feet high, but the gate opened easily, and wasn't locked. No stock, nothing. Only the bleak Huddersfield moors, and a wintry wind that chilled us to the bone. We were first there.

Presently Mrs Hunter's van arrived, and out came Premonition, off lead, at heel, grinning happily; a day out, a big field; people. He moved towards us and up went his head. Puma turned to watch him. Her eyes were glowing, her front legs were bent and her expression was unbelieving.

Is he for *me*?

'Let them play a little,' Mrs Hunter said, and to my amusement added to her dog, 'Be gentle. She hasn't done it before.' He looked up at her, as if he understood perfectly, and began to run with Puma, and to tease her.

I once talked to a man who killed foxes for the farmers. He had killed eight in one day, by shooting, when he saw a dog fox and vixen courting in the snow. He settled to watch. They played for two hours, and he broke his gun, unloaded it, and went home, unable to kill them.

'They were so pretty, I hadn't the heart,' he said, and he was a dyed-in-the-wool, tough-as-they-come professional.

This courtship was the prettiest thing to watch. I always think it is a shame that people today seem to consider sex in anything but the right context as material for idiotic jokes, something to snigger at, something almost out of the ordinary instead of its having been around for as long as there've been mammals; and indeed other creatures too.

To me, it's totally natural. Watching two animals court is the prettiest thing out. They are gentle, affectionate, caressing; they vie with one another, entice one another, no self-consciousness or absurdity about it.

I once watched two seals courting; the big bull was enormous, battle-scarred and ancient, but he was unbelievaby gentle with the little cow, rubbing against her with his head, nosing her, diving under her and over her, playing endlessly in spite of being such a warrior.

And then it happened, and Premonition and Puma were tied. Mrs Hunter held her dog's legs and Puma's, supporting both of them, to keep his weight off the bitch, who is delicately made; I held Puma's head, stroking her and talking to her, as for a moment or two she resisted, panicky and unsure. Then she relaxed. Judy held Premonition's head, talking to him and stroking him. It was run of the mill to him, but he enjoyed being fussed, and was perfectly well used to a public performance.

It is always as well to have witnesses at a mating anyway as pedigrees matter; the wrong dog could be substituted by someone unscrupulous; what you got out of that wouldn't be the litter you hoped for, but something second-rate. And possibly faulty too.

What we hadn't realised was that the dogs had gone into their act right beside the wire fence bordering the road. Lorry drivers slowed and stared, as it must have looked very odd indeed; three crouching women, two mating dogs, and Marian scouting round us to keep off anyone with a dog. It was as well she was there, as right in the middle of the proceedings a man came into the field with a large Alsatian dog. Fortunately he recognised the situation, leashed his animal and went off.

It was all over. Premonition ambled back to his van. I paid the stud fee, and we went home, Puma sleeping as if she'd been drugged.

Now we had to wait again.

Would the mating take?

Or were those frequent seasons the sign of something wrong that might prevent her ever having pups?

It would be some weeks before we knew for sure.

Janus was overjoyed when we came home, and brought me so many presents that I had a small mountain beside my chair. He couldn't get over having been left behind. It was unheard of. And that bitch had been out with me on her own. He didn't approve at all, so that night I left Puma with Kenneth, and took Janus by himself to the dog club.

He was beginning to understand what work meant, but we had a very long way to go, and he was so exuberant, wanting everyone to adore him, as he adored people. It was difficult to remember how shy he had been as a pup; he didn't mind anything now except milk floats. On firework night, when other dogs are in cupboards or under beds, Janus was rushing round the house at every bang, looking for pheasants. The sound of a gunshot and he began to seek; he would bring anything to hand. It was a very busy evening.

Chapter 12

We might be dubious about the mating being successful.
Puma wasn't. She went around looking blissfully happy;
within a week she was even sitting straddled though there
was no sign of a change in her shape. She decided to be in
whelp in style and be sick in the mornings, convincing me
that, whatever some doctors may say, that is *not* psychologi-
cal. No one had told Puma about morning sickness.

She decided she didn't want any dog near her, they
might hurt her pups. So she kept away from Janus and
warned him, gently, to stay away from her. She decided as
she was in such an interesting condition she couldn't
possibly go for long walks, and became a perfect pest as she
needed exercise to keep her fit. Me? Go for a *walk*? In *my*
condition? Victorian madam wasn't in it.

She decided once more to practise maternity on the cats,
to Casey's fury. He seemed to be running forever, turning
against a wall with fluffed fur, swearing, paw slashing.
Puma just laughed. It was funny. Everything was funny.

By the fourth week she was losing her waist, and on the
28th day we went to see our vet. On this day and for
perhaps one or two afterwards it's possible to tell if there
are pups. A vet can feel the heads, like little golfballs. After
that they shift away and no one can tell; which is why if
people are told to take a bitch on the 28th day and they

decide to leave it a day or two longer the vet may well get mad! He's lost the only opportunity he had.

At least six heads.

So Puma was in whelp, but there was still a long way to go. Some bitches start in whelp, and the pups get reabsorbed and disappear. And there was the birth to contend with.

In view of Puma's history of lead poisoning I had decided to let Judy have her back to whelp her. In any case she was entitled to two pups and wanted to use her own kennel name for them, which meant that we had to transfer Puma back to her for the whelping period and then back to me. The Kennel Club works very slowly, so this was going to be a bit of a headache and meant form-filling.

Puma grew vast. She waddled. She lost her lovely sleek figure and was a travesty of a bitch; very pregnant and making the most of it, puffing and panting, sitting so straddled she almost fell on her face, moving with great caution, warning Janus away endlessly. He became disconsolate and lay watching her as if he couldn't understand at all what had come over her. 'Come and play.' 'I've got better things to do.'

So I played with Janus and Puma did long immobile downstays and obviously thought great thoughts, her eyes remote. Come when she was called? She didn't hear. Except for her food plate.

She was ravenous. She was feeding an army and I never gave her enough. She couldn't eat big meals so had to have several mini-meals a day; she had a diet sheet which included vitamins and milk and the occasional egg and everything planned to make the best possible pups. It cost a fortune.

And there was another problem: how can you feed one dog and not another? Put Janus outside and he sobbed; he could smell that food; *she* was having food; *he* wanted food, so in the end I divided his food up into five portions too and he ate when she did, which solved that.

Soon Puma was finding it difficult to get into the back of the Mini; and I didn't want her jumping in case she injured herself. Reluctantly I decided she had better go across to Judy early; she would get used to the whelping kennel and there was then no risk of a mad dash with a whelping bitch in the middle of the night. She was so large our vet thought she would be early.

I took her across. We needn't have worried about settling into the whelping kennel as she had lived there for the first four months of her life; it was home, and she sniffed every corner and settled in the sun. I had seen many whelping bitches lying there; I had never thought to see my own.

I knew too that one had been upset when her owner visited. So I was not going to visit. Judy suggested that when the pups were three weeks old, I come out, put on Judy's clothes, and go in to see them, while Puma was taken for a walk. But I wasn't going to see my bitch for a month.

Janus cried all the way home and kept pawing at me. You've forgotten Puma. Where is she?

He didn't want to play. He worked miserably at the club; but within a few days he was romping again and I spent more time teaching him; the house seemed very empty without Puma.

At Whitsun I went down to the caravan with Janus. Kenneth and the boys went cruising and I walked with the dog and stayed there alone till I realised that campers' children were using the side of my van as a latrine in the night instead of going across to the lavatories.

I was so revolted that on Whit Monday I packed up and went home. It wasn't an easy journey; I developed a steering wobble and going through one narrow little town had to take avoiding action when a sports car overtook without room; the wobble increased and I smashed the rear light of an old heavy car standing in the road, and scraped the whole of one side of my car. The cause of the trouble was well away and I had to explain to the car's owner who luckily was kind. His damage was slight. He was more concerned for mine.

I rang Judy as soon as I got in.

'I was hoping you wouldn't ring,' she said. 'Puma's just starting. I don't want to leave her.'

She rang off, leaving me wondering if I had detected worry in her voice. I began to appreciate in a mild way how expectant fathers must feel.

I took Janus for a walk. I would have to get that car fixed. And I was not very happy at all. I spent a hot restless night thinking of all the things that could go wrong, and remembered the panic I had had only a few days before.

The dogs had been gnawing their bones together, when suddenly Puma flew at Janus, grabbed his bone as well as hers, and savaged it, running round the room with both bones, trying to chew them up, crunching away at them in a manner that could only be described as quite mad.

I rang our vet.

'Calcium lack. Eclampsia. Put her straight in the car, Joyce, and come at once. Don't wait.'

It was nine in the evening. I put Puma in the car and thanked goodness David was only five minutes away. By the time we were there, he had the injection ready. I looked at her eyes. She was staring at me as if she didn't know me and she still had that bone with her. She didn't want to let it go. I got it from her before I took her in.

Two minutes after the injection she calmed down. She came quietly to the car, and lay there, looking at the bone in mild astonishment. The whole thing might never have happened, but David had warned me it might cause

166

trouble again. I had made the mistake of reading it up in Black's Veterinary Dictionary and discovered how serious it is; it can cost a bitch her life. And Puma had already had the symptoms once.

Judy rang in the evening.

All was well. But 'Your bitch,' she said with disgust in her voice.

And then I heard the saga.

Puma had started to whelp just before I rang. When the first puppy came, she gave it one horrified look, and fled to the far end of the corner, staring at it as if it was something from outer space. Touch that? Never.

Judy coaxed her back to the box. Puma had no idea what to do and didn't intend to do it. Judy put her on a 'downstay' and showed her how to clean the puppy up, which she did with the air of a child taking syrup of figs. Ugh!

Clean and tidy, the puppy squeaked and flicked an ear, and Puma nosed it, now interested. At this moment the second puppy came, and she rushed off again. She wasn't doing that again. And she didn't want that little mess beside her nice clean puppy. Persuaded gently that she was a good girl and this was clever, she did her ghastly necessary licking again, and once she had a clean puppy settled down more happily.

The phone rang. (Not me.) Judy left her, and when she went back found a hole in the wooden kennel floor, that Puma had chewed and scratched up, and there at the bottom of it was a very small, drenched and cold puppy.

It was Bank Holiday week, which is a holiday week in the North West, and Judy's husband was home. He was not enchanted to be called from his own jobs to rescue the pup; or to mend the kennel floor. He eyed Puma morosely, remembering that she was the puppy who had stolen his best shoes and buried one in the midden; she seemed to be living up to her past. Joyce's damned bitch again.

Puppies, four, five, six and seven arrived without much incident. Puma wasn't enamoured but she was resigned. Oh well, she had to put up with it. She let them suck for a while, and then, eyes anxious, she began to pace.

Back and forth across the kennel. She should be settled and suckling but she wasn't. And she wasn't acting like any bitch Judy had ever seen.

She rang poor David, on Bank Holiday himself and eleven miles away. He came at once, and examined her, giving her a calcium injection in case it was calcium lack, and another injection to bring on another pup if there was one there, though he couldn't feel one.

She still didn't settle. Five of the pups were fine; well over one pound each in weight and very lively; the fellow that had been through the floor was tiny and obviously extremely weak; possibly Puma knew he was not going to thrive; and one of the little females was also small and not over strong. But five good pups was a bonus. No problem there.

David left, and Judy went back several times to look at Puma, not at all happy about her. On one of her trips a car drew into the yard again, and she found that David had returned.

'I'm not happy about that bitch,' he said.

Puma was still unsettled, restless and uneasy, acting very oddly. He started to examine her, and discovered there *was* another puppy there; an enormous puppy, jammed up under her ribs, not having moved at all. He had to bring it out himself.

It was a beautiful dog pup.

Puma settled soon after that, but the experience had put her off the puppies. The two little ones died and she had to be forced to nurse the others. She wanted nothing to do with them. Luckily I had taught her to 'downstay' so she

168

downstayed and fed them while Judy supervised, having to give her far more time than was reasonable.

I went over to see the pups when they were three weeks old, and crawling. I put on Judy's Wellingtons and mac and gloves and old hat, hoping no smell of me would remain in the kennel. I couldn't bear *not* to see them. Puma was led out well before I was due. I parked my car at the end of the land, so that she shouldn't smell Janus. He had to stay instead of coming to run among the horses, which annoyed him. I was afraid he would howl and she would hear him, but he settled quietly when told, nose on paws, forlorn dog waiting.

I watched the pups crawl around, seeking Puma, wanting milk. Their eyes were open; they were darker than Puma, their muzzles all black, taking after Dad. They were gorgeous, adorable bundles. I wished I had them at home. I made up my mind there and then that I would have the next litter at home, and I spent the next two weeks having a yard built and a trap made in the shed door so that it would be all ready for her. It would be fun to have the pups there, to look after them and to watch them develop; and maybe Puma wouldn't have been so much of a pest if she had been with me; I had more time than Judy for her, and she had now been mine for almost a year.

The entry on Puma's file reads:
Mated March 27th to Champion Rossfort Premonition. (B.OB. Crufts 1974)
Due May 28th.
8 pups born May 27th (4 dogs and 4 bitches).
Dogs named Brora; Balta; Brough; Barra.
Bitches named Shona; Vayla; Skara; Iona.
Brough died May 29th (fluid on lungs).
Skara died on June 3rd—weakly from the start.
Calcium injections given May 18th and at birth.
Abnormally heavy loss treated with antibiotics on 5th day after birth. Very reluctant to mother pups

169

at first; horrified by first three. Then mothered adequately for three weeks, lost interest and had to be forced to continue feeding them.

As a result the pups were weaned early and Puma came home at five weeks after the birth. And were we glad to see her!

Chapter 13

Dogs get under your skin; try as you will, you can't help getting attached to them. I had missed Puma badly. So had Janus. I doubted if she would have missed us. She had been busy with pups and she had been reared at Judy's home, and lived there for more than half of her life. Her time with me had been relatively short.

She had missed us. She raced to the car and jumped in, though she and Janus greeted each other in a remarkably restrained fashion. He sniffed her suspiciously; she smelled alien, of a different place, and she still had a little milk.

I went to look at the pups; they rushed to the wire of the run to greet me, standing on their hind legs, squeaking for attention. They were all bold; they were solid bundles with splendid bone, and I wished I could take one home with me. No matter how I live, I can never have enough dogs.

Judy was going to sell them for me. She, like me, worried about their future homes. No one wants to spend a fortune rearing pups that are going to be mistreated, neglected, or killed under a car before they are a year old. We already had one buyer; a school teacher we both knew had booked Iona. Judy was keeping Balta and Vayla. Balta, a boisterous imp, was now nicknamed Limbo. Two of the pups turned out to have long coats, which invalidates them for showing and meant we had to drop our price. But long-haired GSDs are in great demand for Obedience. There would be no problem there. Judy promised to phone me about every sale.

She has her own method of sorting buyers.

'I want to buy an Alsatian.'

'Well, come and see mine,' and she takes the buyer into the big compound, and releases all her adult dogs that get on well together. If the buyer flinches or runs for cover, he or she is persuaded to try another breed. The German Shepherd is not a dog for timid owners. It needs firm handling and needs to know that Master or Mistress is quite definitely the boss.

The pups were not yet old enough to sell.

I drove home, happily aware that I had all my animals with me again. Kenneth, once more, was abroad; Andrew was out that night too, and I sat watching the dogs. The TV set was on but it was more than normally tedious and the dogs weren't.

They had been very restrained in the car.

They had come into the house quietly, and ignored one another, almost like two shy people, wanting to communicate and not knowing how. Janus, for once, allowed Puma to curl up against him.

They came to me, side by side, eyes bright, tails waving, and Puma pawed me. She hadn't forgotten *that* routine, which was a request for cheese. Both my dogs would go through fire for a piece of cheese.

I gave them each a piece and settled down, but they didn't.

Puma went out into the hall. I glanced at Janus. He was sitting bolt upright, the most eager expression on his face, watching that door, expectant. Puma bounced in, her mouth gaping in her laughing look, bounced up to him, put her paws round his neck and they tussled, delighted to be together again.

The tussle only lasted moments, and then Puma shot out

into the hall again. Again that eager expectant look and in she came and they had their reunion all over again, tussle and all. This went on for almost half an hour. Each time Puma went out, she stayed out longer, teasing the dog; each time she came in their pleasure was more evident, but they were getting excited. Meeting was so lovely that they were trying to repeat the wonderful feeling.

I decided to take them out as soon as Puma came into the room again.

This time Janus was so wildly overjoyed he leaped forward and one of his canines caught in the skin between Puma's ears, tearing an ugly flap. We had a lead walk after that.

The wound itched and Puma scratched. She had become very dirty at night, during her whelping period, probably because the pups were so large, so I did not want to let her sleep indoors. She slept in the outhouse still and day after day I went in to find she had scratched the scab off her injury and it was bleeding.

Inevitably it went septic.

Off we went to David who gave me some red ointment to clear the wound and some blue ointment as she had also managed a fungal infection on top of the other.

'You'll have to put her head in a bucket,' he said. 'I don't like it and it could upset her, especially Puma, but it's going to be necessary or that wound won't heal. And then we'd have bad trouble.'

So I needed an Alsatian sized bucket. I imagined myself going into a shop and trying it on and then I remembered Mabel who managed the hardware shop at the end of the road and had dogs herself, and knew both mine.

I stopped off on the way home. There were several people in the shop.

'I need a bucket for my bitch,' I said.

'This size,' said Mabel, picking up a tool and boring eight holes round the bottom. 'You'll have to cut the

173

bottom out.' Ignoring the astounded faces I took the bucket home, performed the necessary surgery on it, and then attached it to Puma's collar by twists of nylon string. Now came the moment of truth.

I put it on her.

Puma danced; she raced round the room like an idiot, banging against the furniture, trying to knock the horrible thing off.

I caught her, and sat on the floor, holding her tightly.

'Good girl. Good girl'

Not she.

Then I remembered that of all things in the world Puma likes to be funny. Aren't you funny? I say and she cavorts about being a fool. Only when we are alone; she is very dignified in public.

Funny.

The word did the trick. She did a little hula dance, and then settled down. By the end of the day she might have worn her red bucket all her life. People stared when we were out in the car, not only at the bucket, but at the red circle with the blue centre in the middle of her forhead.

Janus, as usual, was very jealous. *He* wanted a bucket.

By now I was beginning to train Puma for Obedience, trying to improve her. Off came the bucket and down it went on the grass, while we worked together. And Janus, blissful, did unasked-for long downstays on the lawn—with his nose inside the bucket, being in fashion too.

We went to one show like that and I was called on the Tannoy to go to the secretary's office.

'This gentleman says your bitch has her head inside a bucket. Is she all right?'

'It took me some time to get the bottom out to put her head in,' I said.

It hadn't occurred to him that the bucket was bottomless though I'm not clear what he thought she'd done. Maybe eaten it!

At Wilmslow some of the dogs looked amazed as Puma came in in her red poke bonnet. They soon accepted it. Just an odd fashion for Puma.

The wound healed and we could soon have the bucket off. By now, owing to the fact that she never learned to gauge distance and invariably bashed the bucket agaainst things, it was in eight pieces, strung around with Sello-tape and looking remarkably tatty.

The last day she wore it I was lunching with Marjorie in Wilmslow and we intended to walk on the disused aerodrome with my dogs and the two Jack Russels, Patch and Scoot. Knowing there was a lot of shrub, I decided we'd keep the bucket on, to protect the newly healed skin from being scratched by thorny twigs.

It was a lovely afternoon; clear and blowy, and the dogs had a wonderful time. Patch found a tree trunk and decided life was incomplete without it. It was far bigger than he was but Jackies are persistent and he did his best to bring it with us.

Meanwhile Puma, Janus and Scoot were playing All Around The Houses through the bushes. Puma raced off at top speed, and we heard the bucket crashing against wood. She returned, grinning, looking totally silly, as the bucket had disintegrated into its eight pieces and was hanging lopsided round her neck, like a huge clumsy necklace. She looked as if she were drunk. She cavorted in front of us.

'Oh, you are funny,' I said, to be rewarded with a beam and a tail wave and paws on my shoulder. We removed the bucket, and she reverted once more to being just dog, not some sort of odd freak that made everybody turn and stare at us.

She was over the pups, but thin as could be, and more worrying, had a brown discharge that went on and on and would not clear up. She had antibiotics and it went; and then returned and David worried lest she became immune to the antibiotics. On the other hand, the discharge

175

obviously made her feel off colour and sometimes made her sick.

We went to the agricultural show at Bakewell. In spite of being only six weeks off the pups, Puma came second in her class.

As summer progressed, she plainly wasn't at all well. We tried a tonic; and we tried vitamins; she had an excellent diet, but she didn't want to play; she would lie quiet for far too long, protest if I tried to take her for a walk and sometimes refuse to walk at all. Dragging her along wasn't my idea of fun; she had more medicine. Now Janus rarely saw David, but Puma was worrying me instead.

Also she had developed a loathing for work; she hated the hall; she wouldn't approach people if they were sitting at the end and she had to go up to them. At the competitions, instead of coming to me, she ran off the floor to Sheila who worked at Judy's and who also went to Wilmslow, although Sheila tried to remain invisible.

By now the pups were sold. One of the dogs had gone to a couple in Didsbury who were thrilled with him; one of the longhairs had gone to someone in Poynton who wanted her for Obedience, and the other, to our pleasure, had gone to replace a long-haired dog that had just died. His new owner was so delighted with him that she sat in the car crying into his coat, refusing to let him go for one second, as he was a replica of her dead dog. Iona had gone to the school teacher we knew. All had excellent homes and I was very happy about them.

Obedience shows that summer were not much good; mainly because I didn't know that there is a vast gap between competition obedience heelwork and the heelwork you are taught at the clubs, bringing a dog in as pet. Competition work is much more like horse dressage; and needs a different training technique, but that as yet was something I hadn't discovered. We weren't awful. We were far from good and Puma was very difficult indeed.

176

Janus was improving all the time but I was worried about Puma's health. She was listless and the discharge kept recurring. I went to a course on training dog handlers to teach pet owners, run by Norman and Rita Hills every year at Totnes. I stayed in a caravan with Brian and Marjorie and the two Jack Russels and my two dogs and we all enjoyed ourselves enormously, except that Puma's discharge was once more so bad that she had to come daily to the vet.

He advised me to see David as soon as I got home, weekend or not.

I raced up the motorway, and rang from Birmingham. David put off his golf and waited in for us. He examined Puma, and gave her an injection, but was afraid she was now immune to antibiotics, and that she had a septic womb.

He saw her on Sunday and asked me to bring her first thing on Monday, and not to feed at all that night. If there was no change, there was only one way to save her life and that was to spay her.

She was far worse on Monday.

I left her behind me, and collected her that evening. I saw her womb; it was full of pus, and I was very lucky to have her. Two other bitches I have known since have died of the same complaint.

It was the end of my dreams of a brood bitch. I couldn't get rid of Puma and start again. I thought of the wasted money on the kennel I had built for her and I cursed, mentally, all the people who still come up and say, 'Who are you mating Puma to next? Can we book a puppy? You had her spayed? What a crime.'

The only crime would have been not to spay her, and to let her die, hoping vainly that she would clear up by magic and produce another litter. Her six living pups are all doing well. Balta, the son that caused all the trouble in the first place is making a name for himself. He is as wilful as

177

Janus and even Eric, who is a big powerful man, finds him a handful in the show ring as he surges forwards, a strong, lusty dog. He has already sired several litters, so we can see Puma's progeny making steps forward too.

I decided to train her for Obedience. Showing seemed to have little point, though I can still show her, as she has a litter registered with the Kennel Club. But somehow Puma and I still had a block. Janus was beginning to be part of a team; he might never do well, but it is hard, now, to believe he was so awful at first. He still tries to get his own way, but he responds far more quickly when I call him, and he is lively, curious, and as full of life as Kym, our Siamese, had been. Like Kym he is too curious for his own good, and sometimes gets into trouble with other dogs by his over friendliness.

I didn't know what was wrong with Puma; not very much, but she just didn't seem to relate to me; she was pleased to see me, but never overjoyed as Janus was.

Then someone suggested that instead of breaking her old associations, I was constantly reinforcing them. We went often to Judy's; met her old kennel mates, and her brother and mother and grandmother; played in the fields she knew so well; and moreover came to Wilmslow Dog Training Club where Sheila goes, and Judy's daughter, Belinda, and a number of Gorsefield dogs.

She should have a clean break and now she was spayed and Judy had two pups, there was no reason why I shouldn't make it.

I left Wilmslow, telling Val why. Both Val and Judy thought I probably had a good point; neither of them had considered it before. Judy suggested that when I visited I left the car down the lane, or left the dogs at home.

It took about four months for Puma to change. At the end of that time, she was a different animal; eager, excited, crying with pleasure when I came home after leaving her, sealing up to me in the morning as she had when little and

I visited the kennels. Completely clean indoors by day and night, so that she now sleeps in the same room as Janus.

I joined the Cheadle Hulme and Cheadle Clubs again, re-meeting Jill and other people I had known. I put Puma back into the nursery class. It gave her confidence and we began to make progress. Janus made immense headway.

There were more competition people than at Wilmslow; I had private lessons from a friend who worked her dogs in championship C; and slowly began to improve. Shows were no longer a nightmare, though Puma seemed accident prone and had several unnerving experiences which didn't help her, due to other people's aggressive dogs.

Then came a new period, in which Janus began to be consistently in the first ten out of fifty competitors at every show we went to, seldom losing more than the odd mark, or half a mark. It gave me encouragement to go on with him, and his rosettes mounted up beside Puma's on another of Kenneth's old ties. His first rosette was a Special from Carlisle Championship show for the Best Gundog; he lost fewer points than any other gundog there on that day and as there were quite a few, I was happy. He also won the Rupert cup; Rupert is a darling, but he is going blind, and having been withdrawn from competition, his owners decided he must make his mark somehow and presented an award in his honour. He is related to Janus, and we meet him often at shows, happily walking beside the Collie that serves as his eyes, using his nose to tell him who is beside him, his tail never stopping its wag.

The cup was a major achievement. My awful dog had brains and could use them. He was delighted with his praise and wagged his tail furiously knowing he had done well.

He had a bonus, a large tin of dog meat, which he carried proudly to the car, while Puma walked beside us, enjoying being out with us and in the sunshine even if she hadn't distinguished herself in the ring.

179

We came fourth, and then third, and then second, and then tied first, though we lost the run off, but it was a great day as we worked under a judge who had seen us before and who came across to say she would never have believed that so much improvement was possible. In her write-up she commented that Janus would have made it if they hadn't started cooking hamburgers right beside the ring just as we passed! Up went his nose to sniff that lovely smell and he went wide, and lost a mark.

Puma had twenty rosettes on the wall from the Open shows. Championship shows only give cards. Janus had seventeen, but we had never yet come first. That happened in one of the club competitions, when we won Beginners, and I was able to add his first bright colour, and there was a shield for Janus on the shelf.

By now life was changing fast, as Nick was married and Andrew about to marry; Kenneth had decided to take the opportunity to become redundant. We bought a summer cottage in Wales and decided to transform it into a new home and move there. There are two acres of ground and it would be better for all of us.

The dogs loved the empty cottage; for one thing it had lots of smells but no furniture, apart from camp beds and deck chairs, as the builders were re-roofing it. They raced round it, delighted to find that rooms lead out of one another so that one dog can come in one door and one at another and still meet. The architecture is so odd that our visitors get lost. We did too, at first.

Kenneth built a new open-plan staircase, keeping the old stairs to act as a ladder. The two staircases were separated by a wall which we removed. One night, when the new stairs were complete and the old stairs about to be discarded, with the floor filled in above them except for one small space, Puma came up to bed behind me and Janus raced up the wrong staircase.

We couldn't find him. We could only hear forlorn whines.

Finally, Puma found him, sitting on the top stair with his head thrust through the floor as if he had been decapitated, quite unable to make out why he couldn't come further. Being laughed at reassured him. He'd done something funny again, though he didn't really know what. He was coaxed down backwards and walked around wagging from end to end, delighted that he'd amused us.

A few weeks later when the new bathroom was being built he discovered a Janus-sized hole to the outside world. The grounds weren't fenced then, the river on the boundary was dry, and there were sheep on the other side. He vanished. We blocked the hole after we had discovered how he got into the grounds.

A large Retriever with a single idea in his mind knows all about blocked holes. He passed the window a few minutes later, so that Puma barked and then oozed up to me, every gesture, saying, 'Aren't I good?' We found he had neatly removed the wood blocking the hole, and gone through again. After that he had to stay on the lead in the house, which was a great indignity, especially as Puma, far more obedient and by now my shadow, coming everywhere with me, lying at my feet, first to greet me in the morning, was able to stay off lead.

In the morning Janus goes to the biscuit box and sits waiting. Puma has to have a private cuddle that no one else sees, and won't touch her biscuit till she's had it.

Moving day was difficult as the animals had to be shut in my car. They watched in amazement during the preceding days as I packed everything into boxes. Twice I went into the garage and discovered that all the dogs' toys and bones and bedding were mysteriously on the floor and not in the box in the kitchen. I removed them and re-packed them and then met Janus industriously transferring the whole lot to the garage again.

In the end the penny dropped. Janus knew something was happening and he and his belongings always *did* come in my car. He was determined they wouldn't be separated, so we loaded the dog gear and he was satisfied. The cat cage was ready, and the vans were due in the morning.

It was our last night and the club competition. I didn't feel like work; I didn't want to move house and had fears for the future in an unknown place, but I did go down.

Janus and I won the Novice cup; a big red rosette and a silver cup to take with us to remind us of the people we were leaving. He knew he had been clever when everyone clapped, and he took the rosette from me, holding it in his mouth, reminding me of one day at a show in the summer when he had quietly snitched a red rosette off one of the tables and I had been startled to find my dog proudly carrying something he most certainly hadn't won.

We had come a long way, the dogs and I, progressing from two anxious animals to dogs I can take anywhere, without too many worries. Puma isn't totally happy yet at Obedience shows, but now we have moved I have begun to handle her myself in Breed, and we are in the cards again, on occasion,

Our first show at our new house was a charity show. We came home with four rosettes. Puma was third in Breed, fourth in the dog with the best coat, and fourth in the dog with the longest tail; Janus was fifth in the dog with the longest tail. We had competition there—Great Danes and a Pyrenean mountain dog! It wasn't exactly show work but it was fun and made money for the mental hospital, whose inmates adored the dogs.

About this time I became a panel member of the new P.R.O. Dog organisation, founded by Mrs Lesley Scott Ordish, who breeds the Trendsett English Setters. My new Saab sports a banner on it saying Dogs Deserve Better People. In small type it suggests joining us and ensuring that rabies never reaches our shores (by educating idiots who try to smuggle dogs in from abroad).

I was asked to go to a school in Egremont, with the dogs,

to give talks to the children and demonstrate with the dogs. They sleep in my hotel room, and take this as a matter of course. We do an obedience sequence on the platform and Janus does downstays while Puma jumps him and works round him. They love being clapped and much prefer being the only dogs there, and the fuss everyone makes of them. We get very few people who don't like dogs.

The round journey was 505 miles, in early December; we had snow, ice, fog, hail, sleet, torrential rain and floods. On the way home the road near Holywell was blocked and I had to make a long detour, when I was pretty well whacked and a little worried lest I were too tired to drive. There is nowhere to stop in winter.

The dogs enjoyed the trip; they had a field to race in next door to the Black Beck Inn, at Beckermet, where we stayed. They came into the bar and the TV room with me, and made friends with a poodle that was staying there. They curled quietly under a table while I ate sandwiches; and they lay behind my chair while I watched TV, ignoring everyone else in the room. One man didn't even know they were there.

They demonstrated beautifully. We were to put on two 'performances', but we ended doing four. Puma found the third tiring and the room was far too hot for her, so that she felt sick and I had to take her out. She stayed in the car while Janus and I put on our last performance at seven-thirty.

I knew he wouldn't work well, as he was bored by now with the process. We had been in the school all day, apart from being taken by the Manessas back to their farmhouse at Gosforth for a truly fabulous meal of goulash and hot French bread and raspberry mousse and cream.

Jill Manessa fed ten people in her big kitchen, had both my dogs inside, as well as her own four-month pup (a Collie cur) and two cats and four kittens. One minute grey scrap had no fear of dogs. Puma had never seen a kitten before. She adores puppies and tries to steal them, recognising the baby smell. Normally she chases strange cats and the two adults and three of the kits took precautions and hid.

Not this fellow.

He sat and stared at her, and she stood over him, enormous, amazed. She had probably never realised cats came as babies too. He was about as big as half of her head, but he was quite unafraid. They remained in that position, amusing all of us, for ages, Puma obviously mesmerised by this baby that was cat baby and not dog baby.

Finally she left him and came to lie at my feet. Janus had been spilled on the floor, nose on paws, for some time, ignoring the pup who who was full of himself and delighted to have dog visitors.

It had been a lot to ask of the dogs, but they did it. On the way home they delighted me even more by behaving so well when we stopped for exercise in the fields at the back of the Motorway services station that an American, whose car was parked beside mine, said: 'What beautifully behaved dogs you have.'

I thought of the long road we had travelled from wild and windy pup and anxious little bitch. The dogs were sleeping behind me, nose on paws, all the way home, ignoring the weather that was bothering me so much.

We now live in a more remote area and Obedience shows are few. The club is delightful but nothing like my competition club where everyone was far more advanced than I and stimulated me to work harder with the dogs. By the end of the summer even Puma was losing only one or two marks in her round, though she still wasn't happy or very good. Janus had been losing about half a mark regularly, which meant he was scoring 99 per cent and over.

I went back to Bolton on November 19th 1976 for their

184

last winter show, staying one night with my son and his new wife and stepchildren and their dog and cat and budgerigar, which fascinated Janus as much as the cuckoo clock did, and the next night with my friend Joy and her two Shelties. All the dogs slept with us, in Joy's room, as she boards students and has no spare room in term time. We had a hilarious night, though the dogs were angelic. Glenn normally sleeps on Joy's bed which I had been given and he didn't think much of the camp bed, so he commuted at first, till he realised I wasn't Joy.

At the show Puma did very little in Obedience but she wasn't there for that. I had put her back in Breed, as the club here is strong on Breed and everyone thinks she is good. Janus came seventh out of sixty in his class, which I thought not at all bad, considering I had had very little time to train him since we moved. He lost 2 marks—there were two bitches in season there.

Puma's show write-up arrived yesterday morning. I rang Judy and she asked if I'd seen it. I hadn't then but delighted her by saying that Puma was going back into the Breed shows. Both Francesca and Carousel are champions now; and who knows?

The judge wrote:

2. Stranger's *Velindre Gorsefield Puma.* This is a lovely bitch teeming with quality. She is short-coupled with hard back. Good front assembly and hindquarters. I thought she would be my winner but she could not match Inka on front reach.'

Judy was especially pleased as Inka is tipped as an almost certain champion, and the comment made of the bitch that came third was that 'she was out of her depth in this company'.

It is so long since we had a show criticism that this one made our day. Puma is due for some local shows, and then will be entered at Manchester, as I cannot face a winter journey to Bolton on January 29th 1977. My Lakeland trip

185

was too hair raising; I was lucky; some travellers on the two days fared much worse.

Janus is improving all the time, eager and happy, wanting to work, so perhaps in the years to come both dogs will go further; it's exciting to plan; and whatever happens, there is a real sense of achievement, as we walk round the lanes, neither dog pulling, Janus no longer flipping at every car, Puma as eager to walk as he, racing to the door when I pick up the leads, racing to the gate to stand impatient, till I come.

We are off for a lesson in show handling and the dogs are lying at my feet, expectant, knowing that soon I will stop typing and it will be their turn.

Upon my wall is a cutting from the German Shepherd magazine in which was Puma's write-up. It is a rhyme on endurance which ends:

'So stick to the fight. When you're hardest hit

It's when things seem worst that you must not quit.'

There were many times when I might have done, but I didn't.

I have learned, even since I started on this book.

Someone I had never met, much more knowledgeable about dogs than I, especially Puma's breed, began to write a book on training the Alsatian. He was put on to me, as being knowledgeable about writing and also as I own one of the breed.

He has been sending me chapters from the book, which I hope will be published at about the same time as this, in instalments; and he has helped me more than he may ever realise.

Dog owners, like many people in all areas of life, are very quick to criticise. Your dog shouldn't do this, or that, or the other; Janus was too thin, too wild, too excitable, and I couldn't control him; Janus was over-sexed, and I should have done something about it; Janus didn't work well and that was my fault, as the handler is always to blame.

Puma was a mess; me again. So people who barely knew us were quick to say.

John Cree, made me think again, and find out more about my critics. I discovered many of them had only owned one dog in their lives, and that not of either of my breeds. They had been lucky with an easy dog without problems and without very much character. The submissive biddable dog is very easy to train; the dog that is one hell of a dog, like Janus, is a major challenge.

I discovered, reading John's manuscript that you learn far more from the difficult dog. That Janus is merely very dominant and not a freak; that his initial problems came from his pancreas and his thyroid trouble and from his being bought as an older pup, not from me. That his awful obedience on Breed show days happens because his sex instinct is still much stronger than his desire to please me. It takes over, and the best handler in the world couldn't fight against that.

None of my guilty feelings were justified. I've turned a horror into an acceptable animal. Sure, he still makes mistakes and can run riot, and so can the most highly trained dog in the Police, given an instinct that overrides his conditioning. I love the story of one disastrous trail. Five police dogs ended at one house. The only 'criminal' was an in-season Boxer bitch!

And then I went on to realise none of my hang-ups with Puma were due to me, either. John's chapter on the Alsatian in the home made me realise I had been misled all along the line by other people, quick to criticise, who knew nothing about the problems. For one thing, John says, it takes months to resettle an older dog, unlike a new pup.

No one could have trained Puma in her early days for Obedience because she was *all* bitch; those frequent seasons and her false pregnancies invalidated that. Her subsequent problems with whelping helped to make her uncertain as she had such a bad time she had been subjected to ill health, which no dog understands, for a remarkably long period. She could, perhaps, have been *beaten* into obeying—but who wants that?

Her flipping at shows was always in the same circumstances; either at indoor shows, or when aggressive dogs were around her. John Cree has trained champions, and judges shows all over the country, and when I mentioned this to him, he assured me his bitch is just the same; she hates indoor shows and aggressive animals around her, and promptly goes to pieces.

He has been working dogs for all his life; and those who do Obedience and who feel as I did, after adverse comment and criticism, that they are failing with their dogs, should get his book on training the Alsatian and reassure themselves. A lot of us have guilts that are unjustified; a lot of us have been criticised by people who don't know enough; who don't have enough experience, and who are full of theories which they never seek to question.

Trouble with a dog is you can theorise all you like, but you never really know. And people are free with suggestions. Make her do it; she is playing you up. Make her do it, she is an Alsatian. Don't force her; play with her.

Judge after judge, all with different ideas; all with different advice; all with different theories.

I felt like the man who took his son and his donkey to market. The old man rode the ass, and people said, 'Look at that old man riding while the young boy walks.' So off the old man got and put his son on and people said, 'Look at that old man walking while the young boy rides.' So they both got on the ass. And people said, 'Look at that poor ass with *two* people on her back.' So off they both got, and fixed the ass's hooves to two poles and carried the ass.

Whatever you do, you can't win.

Theories are all very well. I had a theory as to why Puma chased; racing after anything that moves. I can stop her if I see it first; not if I don't. John's bitch does just the same; is blind and deaf if she sees something fast moving and John doesn't; and reading Leon Whitney the other day, on Dog Psychology, I came across a small paragraph I should have remembered.

The good Shepherd dog has such highly developed guarding instincts that it is a born chaser, after cars, or anything else that moves swiftly; and all that proves is that your dog was bred for the job and would be admirable if it were able to practise in the field for which it is bred.

Just as Janus is forever finding 'pheasants' so Puma is for ever on the *qui vive*, chasing off intruders who menace her flock. She doesn't know they are not eagles or foxes; she only knows that something in her tells her she must protect her territory. She doesn't know we aren't a herd of sheep.

So I endure Janus when he gets sexy and don't ask more than he can perform; if he doesn't win rosettes, he does at least try; his nose may mislead him into a wide or a wander; but I've asked far too much of him; he can no more do what I hope for than I can jump eighteen feet high. I might try but I'd fail!

Similarly I accept that Puma is a splendid guard and she stays on the lead where anything that runs may tempt her. We got into awful trouble this summer when she tried to take off in Heel on Lead in a Show, after stampeding heifers running from a small dog; the judge didn't know about Alsatian instincts and misinterpreted what happened. Small dogs don't behave like big dogs; and every breed and every individual is unique. You can't judge dog and handler other than in the regulation routine in five minutes flat.

So if you hope for laurels in the Obedience field, don't be put off; the professionals are there with carefully chosen dogs, bred for the game; selected for the game, and if they don't succeed, the dogs are often retired or sold. The rest of us have pet dogs and want to train them to be good companions; to see how far we can go in building a team;

man and animal working together, gaining rapport, having fun.

It's easy to become too intense; to be put off by the scathing comments of an inferior judge; the good judges know that people, like their dogs, need to be encouraged; that the worst dog may, in time, prove to outdo all the easy ones. Judges have to learn. They are human too and far from infallible in dogs.

It's easy to feel defeated as you watch other dogs go, apparently so easily, through the routines, but you don't hear about the champion that took eighteen months to learn to retrieve; or the little winning Collie that was so timid she was retired from Shows for two years and then brought back again.

You hear about the clever young dog that wins all his classes before he's a year old; you don't ever see him again, as he's bored to tears and goes stale and can't do the higher classes; you don't hear about the dog that won his first class at eight years old, having been the club booby for all that time.

I have written about my hang-ups, not to excuse myself or my dogs, but because there isn't a dog in the world that is perfect; you can get over some things. We will never get over Janus's fear of milk floats, but he can come with me through London now without flinching; and Puma came to an indoor Show with me last week, sat quietly in a crowd, and we gained two seconds and two thirds in her four classes, competing against dogs of all breeds in a small show, instead of against Alsatians in a big one.

My dogs are young yet; Janus is five and Puma is four. Limbo, her son, is only two; there is a future for all of them. We might go on yet and make her a champion; we might go on yet and win through to higher classes with Janus.

A friend who judges and I were laughing on the phone the other night; no one has ever had a triple Champion, winning in Field Trials and in Obedience and also in Breed. It may be impossible; but I am looking for another pup, and he is looking for another pup, and we both said, 'Why not?' He's much more likely to do it than I as he has so much more experience.

But I dreamed of dogs and I got my dogs; and I dreamed of a brood bitch and I bred a litter from her; years ago I made my teachers laugh by saying I was going to write, and was going to breed pups.

I've done both. So maybe ...

There's all the future ahead of us, yet to be written.

Meanwhile in a moment I will stop typing and turn my head and Puma will be at the door, eager, while Janus bounces round me, groaning, holding his lead.

Come on, dogs, *walk*!